LIVING BEYOND REGRETS

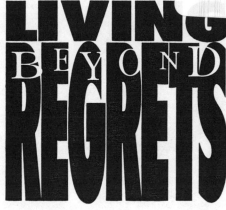

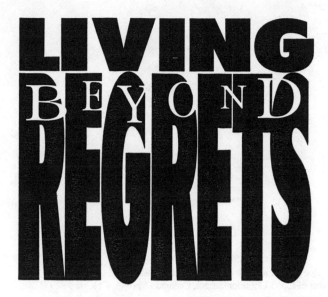

LIVING BEYOND REGRETS

You Can't Change Your Circumstances,
But God Can Change You!

GUY RICE DOUD

Chariot VICTOR
PUBLISHING
A DIVISION OF COOK COMMUNICATIONS

Victor Books is an imprint of ChariotVictor Publishing,
a division of Cook Communications, Colorado Springs, Colorado 80918
Cook Communications, Paris, Ontario
Kingsway Communications, Eastbourne, England.

Editors: Afton Rorvik; Greg Clouse
Design: Bill Gray

Library of Congress Cataloging-in-Publication Data

Doud, Guy Rice, 1953–
    Living beyond regrets / Guy R. Doud
        p. cm.
    ISBN 1-56476-633-0 (pbk.)
    1. Regret—Religious Aspects—Christianity. 2. Doud, Guy Rice, 1953–
3. Consolation. I. Title.
BV4909.D68   1997
248.8'6—dc21   97-25309
                                                                        CIP

"We crucify ourselves between two thieves: *regret* for yesterday, and *fear* of tomorrow."

Fulton Cursler, American journalist

(1893–1952)

This book is lovingly dedicated to my children:
Seth, Luke, Jessica, and Zachary.

Contents

Acknowledgments

Introduction

One   It's Over/13
Two   God, I Can't Do It without You/27
Three   And Jesus Still Loves Me/39
Four   If I Could Turn Back the Clock/49
Five   Failed, But Not a Failure/59
Six   No Fear!/71
Seven   And the Walls Came a Tumblin' Down/79
Eight   Choosing to Rebuild/93
Nine   Come to the Well/101
Ten   The Source of Much Regret/115
Eleven   Regrets and Depression: An Inventory/127
Twelve   Regrets and Depression:
           Further Inventory/139
Thirteen   Never All Alone/151
Fourteen   Come Out of the Cave/161
Fifteen   Getting in Touch with Anger
           and Letting Go/171
Sixteen   A Whole New Way of Thinking/185
Seventeen Kodak Moments/197
Eighteen   Looking Forward to What Lies Ahead/203

ACKNOWLEDGMENTS

There are so many to whom I will be forever grateful, without whose help this book would never have been written, and without whose love I might have chosen to give up. The following people have been Jesus with skin on to me. They have forever reassured me that God is not finished with me yet, and they have reminded me that *the best is yet to come.*

With deep gratitude, I thank the following:

Tom and Deb Isle; Tom Martin; Stephen Gould; Richard Beech; Dale and Ruth Zappe; Barry Sorenson; Shaun Goodsell; Dennis Bird; Linda and Gary Hjelmstad; Peggy Campolo; James Langetaux; Dr. Art Grimstad; Dr. Steven Farrah; Dr. James Dobson and Focus on the Family ministries; David Horton and Greg Clouse; Ruth Geisler, Rick Johnson and others at CPH; Bill Olmsted and Brian DeRosier; Rev. Gordon MacDonald; Don Heidt; Gary Smalley; Rev. Ross Halbersma; my former church family at Christ Community Church, especially Margaret Whitney and Warren Barber; Glen and Carolyn Nygard; Dean and Carolyn Warner; Ray and Carolyn Frisch; Tom and Betty Rosenberger; Jann and Gary Rhubee; Emmet and Helen DeVaney; Eric Klang; Ray and Rose Hope; Fred Peterson, and Family Hope Services; and of course, my family, especially my sisters, Janice and Nicki.

INTRODUCTION

This book is not an autobiography, but it is autobiographical.
I share my personal story with you because I suspect you may have
had some troublesome times, too. Maybe like me, you've gone
from the mountaintop of joy to the valley of despair. Once in the
valley, it is easy to feel so defeated you think the best has passed
you by, and you begin to live a life of regret. Regrets add up and
produce a negative and critical spirit, a life lived in shame and
guilt, depression, and an overall lack of joy. There is a great big
hole in the center of many hearts. Someone has said that "everyone has a Christ-sized hole in the center of their heart."

How can you experience peace? How can you discover real
joy? How can you put failure in perspective? How can you dream
to climb the mountain again? That is what this book is about. It
comes from the deepest part of my heart, and I hope and pray that
it will touch your heart as well.

In Christ's Grip,
Guy Rice Doud

It's Over

Alone in bed, I rolled over and hit the snooze button on my radio alarm. *Another seven minutes,* I thought. The cold, February wind attacked my house, and I pulled the blankets and bedspread over my head and hid, safe in a makeshift cave.

Most of the night I had bargained with God, begging Him to intervene. Had I slept at all? If I had, I sure didn't feel like it.

"It's another coooooooold morning out there, folks, with the wind chill factor at fifty degrees below zero! Be sure to bundle up if you have to go outside." The radio announcer's weather update ended my seven-minute respite,

> **Most of the night I had bargained with God, begging Him to intervene.**

but I just slid under the blankets further. I shut off the alarm. *Why I had set it? It was Saturday. I could sleep in if I wanted.*

As I entertained wishful thoughts of falling asleep, two speeding, giggling children burst through my bedroom door. "It's Tickle Monster time!" yelled Jessica and Zachary simultaneously. Jessica, 6, and Zach, 3, didn't stop to see whether or not I was sleeping, and I was momentarily perturbed. Just as quickly, however, I realized that one day too soon the Tickle Monster would go the way of Puff the Magic Dragon, and so I threw off the blankets and intercepted Jessica with my right arm and Zach with my left.

"The Tickle Monster is going to get you!" I yelled. Their

15

screams were deafening as I held them down and tickled them. Soon their yells attracted Seth, 10, and Luke, 9, who came running to join in the morning's wrestling match.

"Good morning ol' Papa ol' Pal," Seth yelled as he jumped on the bed. Luke lifted a blanket still covering my legs and tried to tickle the bottom of my feet.

"Not my feet! Not my feet! You tickle the bottom of my feet and you die!" I screamed half-seriously, as the kids all laughed with glee.

After a few minutes of this fun roughhousing, we lay exhausted and discovered a rare moment of silence. Zachary, who was on the right side of the bed, was the one to disturb the quiet. "This is where Momma used to sleep," he said.

He had just stabbed me with a sharp dagger.

I took a few moments before I answered: "Yes, honey, that is where Momma usually sleeps."

"She doesn't sleep with you anymore," Zachary continued his observation.

"She hasn't been lately, honey," I said, "but I hope she will again soon."

"Why aren't you and Mommy sleeping together, Daddy?" Jessica asked.

"Probably because Papa snores so loud," Luke said, before he once again began the tickle attack. (I love the way Luke and Seth often call me "Papa.")

"You turkey, Luke!" I forced myself to laugh and continued the wrestling competition.

We were interrupted by Tammy's call from the kitchen: "Kids, breakfast is ready. Come and eat."

Just as suddenly as I had been attacked, the four bedroom invaders headed out the bedroom door and down the stairs to the kitchen, taking their laughter with them.

Alone again, I stared at the vaulted ceiling. A stream of thoughts flowed through my mind, but I chose to dwell on one: *I was glad that Luke had answered Jessica's question.* I pulled the blankets back over me and shut my eyes. *Oh, God, please...* I continued my bargaining from the night before. *Please, God, please!* I screamed in my head. *I can't lose my family, my home! Please, God, intervene, intervene, intervene, intervene* . . . I kept repeating the words over and over again until almost hypnotized, I fell asleep.

Starting the Day

I was awakened over an hour later by the telephone on the nightstand beside my bed. I was surprised that I had fallen back asleep and looked at the clock before answering the phone.

"Hi, honey," my sister, Nicki, said when I answered.

"Oh, hi, Nick."

"I'm in town and I wanted to know whether or not you wanted to join Ann and me for lunch at the Silver Dragon."

Nicki and her friend had driven to Brainerd from Aitkin, thirty miles east. Aitkin, one of many Minnesota towns on the Mississippi River, has been home to Nicki ever since she graduated from Bemidji State University. In Aitkin, she has taught English and German to thousands of junior and senior high school students, and for many years has been pastor of a small community country church. Nicki has been one my mentors, and I am glad she lives close enough so we can see each other frequently, often over lunch. The Silver Dragon Chinese Restaurant is Nicki's favorite place to eat in Brainerd, and she and various friends love to make the half-hour trip and enjoy the Dragon's famous combination plates and other specialties. Whenever I have the chance, I love to join them.

"Ah, yeah, ah, I think I can, but let me check first with Tammy." I jumped out of bed and ran down the stairs, but no one was home. There was a note on the kitchen counter: *"Guy, I am taking the kids to the roller skating rink, and then I'm having lunch with a friend."* I read Tammy's note several times before picking up the phone on the counter and continuing my conversation with Nicki. "Yeah, I guess the kids are going roller skating and Tammy is having lunch with a friend, so what time do you want me to meet you?"

"We're just finishing up at Wal-Mart so we'll meet you at the Silver Dragon at 11:30."

"See you then, Nick," I said. I hung up the phone and walked back upstairs and sat on the edge of the bed. After a few minutes I heard beeping, and I realized that the bedroom phone was still off the hook. *What an irritating sound*, I thought as I slammed it back on the receiver.

I opened the vertical shade to the balcony of my bedroom just in time to see the postman pull up to my mailbox. As a child it always amazed me how the rural mail carrier could drive his car from the right side. I used to believe all these drivers were from England. That thought escaped me, though, as I watched my postman lower his frozen right window, deposit my mail, close my mailbox lid and his car window, before he crawled to a mailbox sixty or so feet north. Exhaust from his car tailpipe formed little white clouds that rapidly disappeared. I stared at the mailbox. Leaning against the window in the balcony door, I took a long, deep breath and exhaled. My hot breath met the cold glass, and the condensation froze, leaving a small patch of crystal. Even though my forehead was pressed against frozen glass, I perspired profusely.

The cold felt good.

I continued to stare at the mailbox. My lawyer had said *Saturday or Monday*. At least I was to be spared the humiliation of having a Deputy Sheriff deliver the papers.

I reluctantly pulled myself away from the window and began my morning grooming and dressing. I looked at my watch and realized breakfast would be lunch with Nicki. Since I'd fallen back to sleep, most of the morning had expired. I now had to hurry to meet Nicki at 11:30.

Thankful and Desperate Thoughts

Frost surrounded the door handle and lined the edge of the door leading from the house to the garage. Adjusting the wool scarf around my neck, I braced for the onslaught as I opened the door. Surprisingly, the cold blast felt good.

The car started immediately, and I couldn't help but thank God for the difference a garage made. Until recently, I had never known the convenience of a garage, I thought. *In Minnesota living without a garage for one's car is like living without insulation for one's house. Yet I've been without a garage most of my life. And my parents were never able to afford a garage. How lucky I am to finally have a garage.*

As I sat contemplating the advantages of having a garage, my garage was filling with a cloud of exhaust.

As I sat contemplating the advantages of having a garage, my garage was filling with a cloud of exhaust. How long does it take before you die? I wondered. *Is it like the gas chambers I've read about? Do you struggle to breathe at the end? Is it similar to Dr. Jack Kevorkian's machine? I thought carbon monoxide was supposed to be invisible? Maybe I see it only because it is so cold? I remember that young couple my policeman father found. . . . And one of my best friends found his father, dead, in the running car, in a closed garage.*

I pressed the button of the garage door opener, and the poison carbon monoxide gas escaped into Minnesota's frigid air. Funny—no—strange, I thought. *Thankful thoughts had led to thoughts of suicide.*

My Buick's tires seemed square as I backed down my driveway into the road. The heater fan squealed as I turned it to high, something it had become accustomed to doing. Shouldn't be that way with a new car, I thought. *How lucky I am to have been able to buy a new car. My parents never were able to afford one. If they were alive,*

I'd buy them one. I was going to take the car to the dealer in November when the squealing first started—still covered by warranty, you know—but then... and now here it is February all ready, and it still isn't fixed! Get on the ball, Guy! Quit putting things off! Of course, most car fans squeal when it's fifty below, but this one squeals even when it warms up.

I heard myself speak and realized I was thinking out loud. My radio was on, tuned to my local Christian radio station. Some kids program, I thought. I inserted the compact disc already in the disc slot. Greg Buchanan's harp tried to soothe me. I cranked the volume almost to capacity. *Drown out the squeaky fan! Saturday or Monday. Get the fan fixed, Guy! The kids. The kids. Oh God, the kids . . . Oh God . . . God . . . Godddddddd!*

The Envelope

I pulled forward to access my mailbox from the driver's side, even though it meant I faced the wrong way on the road. *Saturday or Monday!* I pressed the button that lowered the window. A neighbor retrieving his mail waved at me, and I acknowledged his greeting. *Did he know what was going on in the house across from his? What thoughts his neighbor had just thought, sitting in his closed garage with his motor running?*

Saturday it was.

I could see the thick envelope from my lawyer's firm. Her lawyer had sent the papers to my lawyer who then sent the papers to me. Uninterested in any of the other mail, I threw the bundle of it on the passenger's seat and tore open the envelope from my lawyer. I read the words over and over again:

> *Tamara Ruth Doud, Plaintiff*
> *vs.*
> *Guy Rice Doud, Defendant*

A horn honked and I looked up and saw a smiling neighbor wave as he drove by.

I read the line over and over again that referred to *irreconcilable differences.* Tammy and I had discussed this. I would not agree anything was irreconcilable as far as God is concerned. My face flushed and my heart pounded as I reread those words.

I pulled back into my driveway. I had to call Tom and Debbie, two friends from church, who had been my main support during the last year of uncertainty and struggle.

My tears froze during the walk from the driveway to the house.

"Remember what your doctor said, Guy," Debbie said, referring to the counsel I had received from a Christian psychologist. "This is not an insurmountable tragedy. You'll go on. Time heals. God promises the best is yet to come. You still have your gifts and talents. Your children will always be your children. God hasn't given up on you, Guy."

I had shared my psychologist's counsel with Tom and Debbie, but I wasn't sure I believed it, let alone accepted it. At this moment I could think of no greater tragedy than going through divorce when still in love.

> "This is not an insurmountable tragedy."

The psychologist had said: "If one of your children were killed in an accident, that would be a tragedy. If you were stricken in some way where you could no longer use the talents and gifts God has given you, that would be a tragedy. If you found yourself without friends and without God, that would indeed be a tragedy. You are losing something, yes, but there is so much more you can gain and nothing stopping you from gaining it. This is not a time to lose your faith, but rather a time to use your faith!"

How many sermons had I preached on exercising faith in the midst of adversity?

It is far easier to preach it than it is to live it.

Tom got on the phone and in his fashion simply said, "You gotta hang in there, brother." And I knew he was speaking from experience. "You've known that this day would come. Now you can start getting on with the rest of your life."

Not quite yet. I still clung to the hope that as long as the divorce was not final, there was still a chance. Like a man receiving a diagnosis of terminal cancer, I found myself going through all the stages of death and dying. The divorce papers I had just read had momentarily broken my denial, and although I was to do more bargaining, I was beginning to experience great anger.

For years I had often allowed my Irish temper to flare out of control, and I usually justified my rage by claiming it was genetic, or "righteous indignation." My anger had at times seriously affected my Christian witness. Preach a sermon about love on Sunday and shout at a waitress who didn't meet my expectations on Monday. Tammy had told me she was sometimes afraid to approach me about a problem or disturb me while I was working. Concerned friends and some people in positions of church leadership had confronted me about my behavior. For over two years I had been receiving counseling, discovering the source of my anger, and working diligently at anger management. Those who cared and were involved told me that they had noticed a tremendous positive difference.

So how could I work through the anger surrounding an impending divorce and not sin? I did not yet have the answer, and quite frankly, at that moment I didn't care. As I hung up from talking to Tom and Debbie, despite their perceptive words and counsel, I wasn't thinking about controlling anger as much as I was worrying about the future, about my worth to God as a divorced person, about my career, about my children, about my survival.

So, the day had finally arrived. It had been three years since Tammy told me she no longer loved me. I had bargained. I had pleaded. I had begged. I had begged Tammy. I had begged God. I had begged others to try to help. In the past, whenever I faced a problem I knew there was always a solution. Somehow I had always been able to scheme, plot, plan—manipulate the situation to my desired outcome.

But, I thought, *I have changed, and I keep asking God to help me to continue to change! I've come a ways and I have a ways to go!*

Tammy saw my change as just another attempt at manipulation. Hurt too badly by some of my previous behavior, and convinced I was incapable of any real change, Tammy gave up on me. She refused to seek Christian counseling with me. I would manipulate the counselor, she said. I would make her out to be the bad guy. The bottom line was she no longer loved me, she said, and believed she never could again. She simply wanted out.

My Regrets

For years I have heard people say you can't really know God's love unless you love yourself. I've always thought it should be the other way around: you can't really love yourself unless you know God's love. No deep theological digression here, but at this moment, I hated, not loved myself.

It would be easy to make Tammy the scapegoat, to blame her for giving up on our marriage. After all, I was willing to do anything possible to make the marriage work. I had admitted my faults. I had been willing to change. I didn't want to give up, *Tammy* did. Nonetheless, I was nauseated, believing that if I hadn't been the way I was, I wouldn't be facing divorce.

> **I was nauseated, believing that if I hadn't been the way I was, I wouldn't be facing divorce.**

But was I responsible for the way I'd been? Wasn't I a product of my dysfunctional past? Yes, to both questions. Even though my family history explained why I had such anger, such need for recognition and acceptance, my family history did not absolve me from my responsibility as a Christian. But how can one change before he realizes change is necessary?

At this point I realized my life was filled with a million regrets—

If only I had . . .
I wish I would have . . .
I wish I wouldn't have . . .
I could have . . .
I should have . . .
I can't believe I did . . .
I can't believe I didn't . . .
If only I could . . .

Regrets. And unlike Sinatra's song, I've had more than a few, and most of them have come from doing it "my way" rather than God's way. I had to accept my responsibility—the fact that my sin had led to the breakdown of my marriage. It mattered not whether I thought Tammy had legitimate grounds for divorce. (I did not.) What mattered was that I accept responsibility for my sin.

Because of my wholehearted repentance, I had been forgiven, yet sin still has consequences. With this knowledge the floodgates of regret were opened as wide as they could open.

A Kind Gift

The phone rang. I was still standing in the kitchen where I'd hung up the phone from talking to Tom and Deb.

"Hello."

"Honey, are you coming? We've been waiting."

It was Nicki calling from the restaurant. I didn't feel up to meeting her and her friend for lunch, but the words that came out of my mouth betrayed me: "I'm sorry. I'm on my way now."

Nicki had been aware for many months that Tammy was threatening divorce, but she wasn't aware of recent events. As I entered the Dragon, she extended her usual smile and hug, as did her friend, Ann.

"I have a little Valentine's gift for you, honey," Nicki said, handing me a package.

"What's this?" I asked, surprised and relieved she hadn't asked me why I was so late.

"A little something I know you want."

I unwrapped the gift, a pair of Minnetonka moccasins with rubber soles. "Oh, Nicki. Thank you so much. Where did you find them? I've been looking all over for them."

Nicki explained, and I again expressed my appreciation for her most thoughtful gift, but I couldn't bring myself to tell her about what I had just received in the mail. Maybe if she had been alone, but then again, not in public . . .

I don't remember much more about that meal and our time together, except later Nicki told me that it seemed as if I had been in a trance. She and Ann had assumed I was just tired.

Final Words

I was home before Tammy and the kids came home from lunch and roller skating. The children were oblivious to what had happened. Tammy and I had both talked with them about divorce, but now that I actually was being sued I experienced a new level of anxiety.

I was sitting at my desk when Tammy entered the office off the living room and asked, "When are you leaving for the convention?"

"I don't feel like going."

Silence.

"I got the papers in the mail this morning, Tammy," I said and then began to weep almost uncontrollably. At that moment I would have given my life itself if she had wrapped her arms around me and told me there was still hope.

Tammy was uncomfortable with my display of emotion, and perhaps I mistook her discomfort for vulnerability. I began to beg all over again.

"Quit making it so hard on yourself, Guy," she said. "We've been over this a million times and nothing is going to change."

"I won't give up hope!" I shouted though my tears. "God can still work a miracle!"

"Then He'll have to do just that," Tammy replied. "It's over, Guy. It's over."

She turned and walked away.

God, I Can't Do It without You

The fellowship of Christian friends sustained me through the next few weeks. When I wasn't with my children, I spent most of my time at Tom and Deb's. They cried with me, prayed with me, fed me, hugged me, and continued to assure me that God was still in control. Sometimes we just sat without exchanging words.

God also provided me with a network of Christian friends all over the United States. I built up quite a phone bill calling Steve and Dick in Pennsylvania; Dale in Arizona; Shaun, Barry, and Dennis in Minneapolis; and James in Virginia. And when I didn't call them, the Holy Spirit seemed to let them know when they should call me. These friends, along with many local friends, didn't realize they were my lifeline at this time. Not only were they there for me in the days immediately following my receipt of the divorce papers, they have been there ever since.

One day my insurance agent, Bill Olmsted, called me concerning my life insurance policy. I had known Bill for many years. He had experienced some very significant challenges in his personal life. These struggles, some would call them failures, had brought Bill very close to Christ. He became very active in his church and in Promise Keepers. When he heard my voice on the phone, he said, "You shouldn't be alone." He and his partner, Brian, took the rest of the day off from work, brought over submarine sandwiches, and spent hours with me.

Gradually I was moving beyond denial, but moving beyond denial meant I was swamped with a million regrets.

Begging for a Miracle

Nonetheless, I still kept bargaining. I had read about the Brooklyn Tabernacle's twenty-four hour prayer choir, and I sent them a letter requesting continuous prayers that God would work that miracle Tammy said she needed. I called churches that I knew had prayer chains, and I asked to have us included in their prayers.

I soon came to realize, and some friends tried to tell me in the kindest way, no one could fix my problem for me.

I thought of Gary Smalley, whom I had met at Bill and Gloria Gaither's Praise Gathering of Believers. Gary's ministry focus is mainly on spousal relationships and the family, and so I hunted Gary down between planes at Denver's Stapleton Airport. Once I got him on the phone, I quickly tried to sum up the situation for him and prayed maybe he had some magic solution.

I soon came to realize, and some friends tried to tell me in the kindest way, no one could fix my problem for me. There were many who were willing to "be there for me," but they couldn't be me for me. There were no magic solutions.

Thinking in Las Vegas

A few days after receiving the divorce papers in the mail, I found myself in a plane on my way to a convention in Las Vegas, the one I had told Tammy I was unsure I would attend. I was to be a keynote speaker for the National Association of Secondary School Principals. Although I was very honored to address this group and had been looking forward to it for over a year, I had to force myself to go. Performing artists occasionally cancel concerts listing "exhaustion" as a reason. Couldn't I do the same? If I skipped the convention and stayed home, maybe I could figure out a solution to "make life good again."

Truth and reason finally won out. I would attend the convention. It was an opportunity I could not pass, and it would afford me some very valuable exposure to educators from all over North America.

Also, Focus on the Family, with whom I had published two books and made three videos, was going to have a booth at the convention publicizing my school videos and other products they had available for public schools. I had told them I would be at the booth during the convention.

Ironic, I thought, Focus on the Family, and I'm going through a divorce. I had been up front with those in positions of leadership at Focus on the Family, and they were aware of Tammy's intentions to proceed with a divorce, although they were not yet aware that she had actually filed papers. I feared a divorce would render me useless for service to ministry.

I certainly did not want to cast aspersions on any ministry, and for that reason had taken a leave of absence from the church I served as pastor. I felt that I had done nothing to disqualify me from serving God as a pastor. Others felt differently. As I examined the whole issue of integrity and accountability, I could see that the Bible was very clear about most things, but some things depended on various interpretations of Scripture. Many of the denominations have something different to say about who can stand in the pulpit.

Discovering I still intended to conduct a public ministry, one pastor rebuked me so severely that I thought myself the devil incarnate. According to him I should not even identify myself as a Christian. When I challenged him concerning the qualifications necessary to serve the Lord, he painted a person so perfect Christ Himself would have had a hard time qualifying, what with His display of temperament when He drove the money changers from the temple, and considering the fact His mother was pregnant before she was married. Those things had certainly affected HIS reputation.

Eventually I came to the conclusion I could never please

everyone, nor did I have to please everyone. I had to please God. I sought God's heart, will, and direction for my life. I sought accountability and surrounded myself with a group of respected Christians to whom I gave permission to ask of me whatever they wished. I listened to their counsel and at times, their rebuke. But they all assured me God wasn't finished with me yet.

As I looked out the airplane window at the billion lights of Vegas below, I asked God to help me believe it.

Valentine Cards and More Regrets

The taxi took me to the Hilton. I greeted a life-size statue of Elvis as I walked to register at the front desk.

After checking into my room in what was once the largest hotel in the world, I found myself in the hotel gift shop looking at Valentine cards. I picked out one for each of the kids, but what about Tammy? I picked up one that said "To my Sweetheart. . . ." Denial shouted to me and then sang a pretty tune. There still was a chance . . .

The clinking clanking sound of the hotel slot machines beckoned me to come give a pull for a million dollars and a new life. But I had new life in Christ, didn't I? Didn't Scripture say that "if anyone is in Christ, he is a new creation; the old has gone, the new has come"? (2 Corinthians 5:17) If I was a "new creation," why did I feel so old? Can you become new again after you've already become new again? My mind raced with similar questions before I put the Sweetheart card back on the rack.

> **I sought accountability and surrounded myself with a group of respected Christians to whom I gave permission to ask of me whatever they wished.**

Regrets. They destroy the abundance and joy of new life.

Regrets. They are some of Satan's most subtle darts.

Regrets. They result from unfulfilled expectations, when things don't turn out the way we planned.

It is one thing dealing with the regrets from our lives prior to our life in Christ, but even after we become Christians, things still don't always turn out the way we planned. Christians are not immune from the "I wish I would haves..." and the like. But what impact do we allow regret to have in our lives? Do we become *paralyzed* by regret, or *propelled* by regret? Do we *lose* our faith, or do we *use* our faith? Key questions.

My experience in counseling hundreds of struggling souls, and my personal experience, is that with added regret comes loss of self-worth. When failure occurs as a result of our inability to control all we wish to control, as inevitably it will, we are crushed. Our pride is deflated, and we suffer from lack of self-worth because we've failed to "measure up" to our expectations, or what we perceive to be others' expectations for us.

Since we were children there have been expectations for our lives. Parents often project their expectations on their children. "My child is going to be a doctor, a star basketball player, a concert pianist...." "My child is going to get good grades in school, avoid drugs and alcohol, remain sexually pure and morally straight."

Then we enter into the community and we face another whole set of expectations. Schools set expectations. Churches have expectations. The government has expectations. And our friends have expectations. Many of these expectations are good, but when they are unfulfilled, they often result in regret for both those who held the expectation and for those who were unable to meet the expectation.

Then there are those whose regrets lead them to rebel, thumbing their nose at God and turning their backs. Like the prodigal son, they take all their father's inheritance and squander it away on riotous living.

The Depth of My Sin

I sat in my room at the Hilton and wrote the following question in my journal: "Did I choose to rebel, or had I simply failed to meet my expectations?" The latter would absolve me more easily of my guilt, but as I explored the question on paper I realized I was unable to let myself off the hook. In a real sense, I had chosen to rebel against God. I was born with a rebellious nature. Just as Adam and Eve rebelled, I had rebelled. I had reached for forbidden fruit and enjoyed its sweet taste while God wept. I had failed not only to live up to my expectations and others' expectations, but I had also failed to live up to God's expectations.

I had always been ready to admit I am a sinner, but I realized that night, sitting alone in the Las Vegas Hilton, I had always viewed my sin as rather inconsequential. I had always been a "fine young man," a Scripture reciter, a Four Spiritual Laws distributor, a church pillar, and somehow in my eyes that made me less of a sinner than others.

I began to weep at the reality of the depth of my sin. Never before had I been so convinced that I really was a "miserable sinner." How many times had I sung the verse of one of my favorite songs, "Amazing Grace, how sweet the sound that saved a wretch like me?"

Without exaggeration, I bet I had sung that song 10,000 times, and yet never believed I was really that wretched. But the last few days had convinced me otherwise.

I had even preached about how John Newton, the slave-trader turned hymn writer, who had written those words I loved as well as the following words: "I once was lost, but now am found, was blind but now I see!"

It had always been easy for me to see how John Newton could write these words. A seaman by trade, he had become engaged in the despicable practice of capturing natives from West Africa to be sold in slave markets around the world. After a perilous, near fatal storm at sea, he began to read *The Imitation of Christ* by Thomas à Kempis. The Holy Spirit ministered to Newton, and he became a devout follower of Jesus Christ and a minister of the Gospel. One Sunday, this man with new vision proclaimed loudly: "I am a great sinner and Christ is a great Savior!"

I knew I had done nothing as horrific as John Newton, but was John Newton's confession simply of those sins committed before he became a Christian? Is there a need for us to acknowledge the depth of our sin even after we come to Christ?

Since that night in Las Vegas, I've read more about John Newton. Once he became a Christian, his struggle with sin did not cease. He wrote: "I am, in myself, incapable of standing a single hour without continual fresh supplies of strength and grace from the fountain-head."

I lay in bed but could not sleep. Why is it so many Christians I know try to convince the world they are perfect? I had fallen into that trap.

> There were so many areas of my life, the life I thought to be a committed Christian life, still so filled with pride and sin.

We don't want anyone to know we're struggling with envy and pride. Worse yet, perhaps, like John Newton, we're blind, and we don't even realize we are lost and going the wrong way. There were so many areas of my life, the life I thought to be a committed Christian life, still so filled with pride and sin.

Oh, I understand the theological doctrine of grace. I am not saved by jumping through all the right hoops and leading a sinless life. I am simply saved by grace through faith by the shed blood of Jesus Christ.

But guess what? I expect—and know others expect me to jump through all the right hoops anyhow. And I can't. . . . I just can't. Unfulfilled expectations. Shattered dreams. A broken heart. And wheelbarrows filled with regrets.

That night I finally realized my greatest challenge: admitting my inability to always win, to always be first, to always come out on top. I've come to call it self-lust. That sounds rather generic, perhaps rather tame, not too shocking, but think a minute. To gain victory over self-lust one must crucify his or her pride, the most deadly of all sins. It is pride, self-lust, which leads us to believe we have all the resources necessary to succeed. We must learn to say with John Newton: "I am, in myself, incapable of standing a single hour without continual fresh supplies of strength and grace from the fountain-head."

I turned on the light and took the divorce papers out of my briefcase. They lay under the four Valentine cards I had bought for my kids. John Newton couldn't stand a single hour without a fresh supply, well I couldn't stand a single minute.

Struggling to Completely Trust God

I held the papers and thought it ironic God would allow them to break me. Oh, I believed I had experienced brokenness before. I had, but I had not been broken completely. I believed I had given up and surrendered before. I had, but not completely. I believed I was an important passenger on God's celestial bus. I was, but I kept wanting to drive.

I recalled a story I had recently heard. The story involved a man who decided to learn to walk a tightrope. He strung a rope in his backyard and practiced each day for many hours. His neighbor watched intently as the man fell repeatedly into the net below, only to get back up and try again. As the days passed, the neighbor noticed his tightrope-walking friend was becoming quite accomplished. Then one day the neighbor noticed his friend was walking without a net. "Good work!" he yelled to the man on the rope, who was now confident enough to wave back.

As the days and weeks of practice continued, the neighbor noticed how his friend kept raising the tightrope and extending the distance from pole to pole. He was amazed at how rapidly and how far his friend had progressed. Then one day he saw the man standing on the tightrope platform with a wheelbarrow. "What are you going to do?" he called curiously to his neighbor.

"I am going to walk the tightrope pushing the wheelbarrow in front of me!" the daredevil answered back. "Do you think I can do it?"

Without a moment's hesitation his neighbor answered, "I'm sure you can! I've been watching you for weeks now. You are wonderful! I have complete faith in you!"

"Glad to hear it," said the man. "Come get in the wheelbarrow!"

Of course, the neighbor refused. So much for "complete faith."

I had heard this story in a spiritual twelve-group I attended. I believed I had given up completely and jumped in God's wheelbarrow.

> **"God, I finally realize I can't do it! I believe You can, but I'm not sure I trust You enough to let You do it."**

Now I realized that I had been chicken, untrusting. Even with this insight, I wasn't sure I was truly ready to give up and get in. But I had become quite convinced I could no longer do it alone.

One of the other guys in our support group, a recovering alcoholic, shared the turning point for him was when he got to the point where he finally screamed "I can't do it! God can! I'll let Him!"

Prostrate on the floor of my hotel room I cried out to God: "God, I finally realize I can't do it! I believe You can, but I'm not sure I trust You enough to let You do it."

It was an honest prayer, and it provoked a release of deep emotion. Not trust God? If I couldn't trust God, whom could I trust? And yet I had been unwilling to trust God completely. I hadn't wanted to get in the wheelbarrow.

I thought about my daughter, Jessica, and her initial fear of climbing on our snowmobile with me. She had panicked and literally thrown a fit, refusing to go. I remember yelling at her over the roar of the loud Polaris motor: "What's wrong, honey? Don't you trust me? Do you think Daddy would do anything to hurt you?"

All Jessica could answer was, "I don't want to go! I don't want to go!"

"Please, honey! You'll love it! You can trust Daddy!"

"I don't want to go! I don't want to go!"

I didn't make her go, and God wouldn't force me to get in the wheelbarrow either.

It was early in the morning before I finally fell asleep, dreaming of wheelbarrows.

And Jesus Still Loves Me

The phone startled me. I sat bolt upright, unsure of what time it was or where I was.

"This is your 6:30 A.M. wake up call, Mr. Doud. Have a good day."

"Yeah, ah, thanks . . ." was all I could manage. At least it had been a real, live person and not a recording. I rubbed the sleep from my eyes, reached for my glasses beside the bed, and surveyed the room. The thick stack of papers stuck halfway out of my briefcase. "Doud vs. Doud."

"Oh, yeah . . ."

All the feelings of last night came back to me in a moment.

Asking God for Assurance of His Love

I sat up in bed and tried to psyche myself up to go give a keynote address. I picked up my copy of *My Utmost for His Highest* and read the daily devotional. The Scripture reference was from Philippians 2:17, and the title of the day's devotional was, *"Are You Ready to Be Poured Out as a Drink Offering?"* Chambers asked several questions I also asked myself: *"Do you say 'I don't want God to tell me how to serve?'" "Are you ready to be a doormat, or do you need to be the hero?"* I thought for a moment. *I prefer being the hero, thank you very much.*

Pride! Self-lust.

I read Paul's words, quoted in the devotional: *"But even if I am being poured out like a drink offering on the sacrifice and service coming from your faith, I am glad and rejoice with all of you."* It amazed me how the Holy Spirit used Oswald Chambers to write some-

41

thing that always blessed me, even though at times it infuriated me. I laid back down in bed, and stared at the ceiling.

"Lord, I want to get in the wheelbarrow, I want to trust You like Paul trusted You, but I need some assurance that You still love me."

Was it really God's love I doubted? Or my lack of love for God? Coming to grips with the reality of my sin, my utter depravity, had left me with so much guilt, and so many regrets. How could I get beyond all the regrets?

> **"Lord, I want to get in the wheelbarrow, but I need some assurance that You still love me."**

A dear Christian friend used to tell me that the longest distance in the world is the eighteen inches between the head and the heart. So true. In my mind I knew of God's love, Christ's unconditional agape love, the Spirit's constant comfort and presence, but in my heart, filled with guilt and regret, I was unable to accept it. In my mind I could say "Jesus loves me, still," but my heart shouted, "How could Jesus love me?"

I restated my earlier prayer, "God, may the knowledge of my mind become the reality in my heart."

The Pain Behind the Stories

After some time I dressed and headed for the convention center. I was early, but I wanted to scope things out and see if I could find the Focus on the Family booth among the exhibitors. I walked the short distance from the hotel, through the lobby filled with slot machines, crap and blackjack tables, and a brand new car Corvette sitting on a pedestal waiting to be won.

I said "Hi" to Elvis, who remembered me from yesterday.

"Excuse me," said a man in a business suit. "But aren't you Guy Doud?" He was with several other men and a woman who were all wearing NASSP name tags—conventioneers.

"Pleased to be recognized, I said, "Yes I am," and held out my hand to greet him and his friends. "And you are?"

He introduced himself. He explained he had heard me speak to a group of secondary school principals in Pennsylvania, a year earlier. "You're really going to love this guy," he told his friends. "When I heard him speak, I never laughed so hard in my life. He had me laughing one moment and crying the next."

It always feels good to have your ego massaged.

"Are you going to tell the jockstrap story?" he asked.

The jockstrap story, as the principal called it, is the story I tell that people seem to remember most. The story recounts my first day of seventh grade, and my first experience in physical education class. My drill sergeant-like physical education instructor ordered all us trembling seventh graders, most of whom had never undressed in front of anyone, to "hurry up and get your jockstraps on!" I had never worn a jockstrap, and when I took mine out of the box that said *Bike*, I saw the tag, and assumed, as with all other items of clothing, the tag went in the back. I soon realized, however, that this "supporter," as it was called on the box, was not supporting anything. By the time I realized it, it was too late.

"Look at this," the teacher shouted. "Fat boy doesn't even know how to put on a jockstrap." His ridicule was good for a big laugh from my classmates but left a permanent scar on my confidence and self-worth. Over the years the scar has healed, but a scab remains, and sometimes the scab gets picked off, opening the wound again.

Even though this story is about one very painful moment in my life, everyone loves to laugh when they hear it.

"Yeah, I'll probably tell the jockstrap story," I answered.

"Well, you better," said the principal. "I've been telling everybody how much they're going to enjoy you."

"Thank you very much," I said. "I hope I don't disappoint you."

"What about that other story you tell . . . how does it go?"

Something about you being your kids' uncle, or something?" The Pennsylvania principal had no idea I was still trying to decide whether or not to tell that story.

When I speak, I often explain I don't have any real claim to fame. One novel thing about me, however, is I didn't have my first date until I began my second year of teaching. Then I started going seriously with a girl named Tammy. We went together for several years before I got up enough confidence to ask her to marry me. Once we decided to get married, I thought our parents should meet each other and approve of our upcoming nuptials. *I'm old-fashioned,* I always explain. Well, Tammy's mother was divorced, and my father was widowed. I invited Tammy's mother and my father to my house for dinner. And they hit it off. Tammy and I were married in June and our folks were married the following August.

> **How could I tell a bunch of strangers I was in the process of a divorce?**

I then explain that marrying Tammy and the fact our parents married each other made my father my father-in-law, my mother-in-law my stepmother, and my wife my stepsister. Our children, three boys and one girl, are actually our nephews and our niece, and I'm my children's uncle.

I explained the story to the principal and his friends, and they laughed uproariously. Then I said: "I'm not sure yet whether I'll tell the story or not. I'm limited for time."

"Oh, you have to tell it," several of the other principals said.

How could I tell a bunch of strangers I was in the process of a divorce? This question to myself served notice to me I was coming to a greater acceptance and reality of where I was in my relationship with Tammy. I still wanted to live in denial, but I knew to move beyond regret involves coming to terms with reality. I thought of the saying on a T-shirt one of my twelve-step groups members used to wear: "Denial Isn't a River in Egypt."

"We'll see," I said.

The group from Pennsylvania told me they would be looking forward to hearing me. I told them "thanks" and "good-bye" and continued down the hallway.

A Shoe Shine and God's Assurance

I left the Hilton and walked outside the short half-block to the convention center. Amazing. Seventy degrees above zero here, thirty degrees below zero at home in Minnesota. I stopped a minute to soak in the desert sunshine before entering the big building. I sure didn't feel much like giving a speech.

I hadn't gone far into the building before I heard someone call my name, "Mr. Guy," he said, "how about you get those shoes shined?"

I looked to my right and saw a shoeshine man, standing beside his chair in the lobby of the convention center, waiting for his next customer. *He didn't know me,* I thought, *he must call everybody Mr. Guy.*

I had no intentions of getting my shoes shined. I remembered how just a few months earlier Tammy and I were in New Orleans for a life insurance convention I was to address. We were leaving our hotel on our way to a nearby restaurant when a young boy came running up to me, shoe polish and rag in hand, and began to give me a free polish. As he worked on my wing tips he said, "For ten dollars I bet I can tell you where you got yore shoes."

"What do you mean?" I asked, dumbfounded.

"I can tell you where you got yore shoes."

This guy from Staples, Minnesota (me) was so naive that I figured the kid was an expert at shoes, and by polishing them he could somehow make a guess at where I had purchased them. I decided to risk ten dollars. There was no way he was going to say "Herbergers in Baxter, Minnesota."

"All right," I said. "Where did I get my shoes?"

He laughed and answered, "What I said was I bet you ten

dollars I could tell you where you got yore shoes, and you got yore shoes on yore feet. Now give me my ten dollars!"

I have since discovered that this is a common ruse, used by street pranksters worldwide, but I had to learn by experience. I gave the kid five dollars and thanked him for the shine. He didn't protest but thanked me and ran off to pull his trick again. As Tammy and I walked away, I heard him say to some other potential guinea pig, "I bet I can tell you where you got yore shoes," but this guy just said, "I have them on my feet. Get lost, kid."

That entire incident flashed through my mind, and I was still reliving it when the old gentleman before me asked again, "Mr. Guy. Why don't you let me shine your shoes?"

"Oh, uh . . . " I said, looking down at my shoes. "Can you make these shoes really shine?"

With a pumpkin smile and lantern eyes he nodded his head and answered affirmatively, "Better'n new, mister! Better'n new!" He reminded me of Louis Armstrong, although he had to be considerably older. I guessed him in his late seventies. His face was like a raisin, and his cheeks shined like my shoes would when he finished them.

I climbed up into the elevated chair, and he helped lift my feet into the stirrups. He wasted no time setting to work. He grabbed the cordovan polish and applied it to my wing tips, not bothering to use a polish applicator, only his hands. I watched him work the polish into the cracks and crevices in the leather.

How many shoes had he shined? I wondered. How many thousands of times had he bent over someone else's shoes? Was he working for a little extra money, or did he need this income to survive? I felt a strange concern for this man and didn't know how to express it. Finally, I asked, "How are you doing?"

"Almost done, mister! Almost done!" He almost sang his answer.

"No, I don't mean how are you doing on *my* shoes, I mean how are *you* doing?"

He stopped buffing for a moment, raised his head, and his eyes met mine.

"How are *you doing?*" I asked again.

"Well, mister," he said, "let me put it this way. I woke up this morning, and my heart was still beating. I got out of bed, and my legs was still working. I went to the kitchen and opened the refrigerator, and it was still running. There was food in the refrigerator, and Jesus still loves me."

"I woke up this morning, and my heart was still beating. There was food in the refrigerator, and Jesus still loves me."

Most people think I'm exaggerating when I tell them that his eyes filled up with tears when he mentioned Jesus, but they did. Really.

And so did mine.

If Only I Could Turn Back the Clock

God used that old shoeshine man to bridge the distance between my head and my heart. There was no doubt in my mind that God still loved me. Jesus hadn't given up on me. The Holy Spirit still filled me. God would help me go on, *beyond regret.*

Longing to Turn Back the Clock

I thought of a woman I had counseled. She had buried her face in her hands and cried: "If only I could turn the clock back one day, my life would be so much better." She went on to explain a number of poor choices she had made. A recovering alcoholic with several years of sobriety and several medallions to show for it, she had decided to drink "just a little bit." A *little bit* led to *a lot.* She ended up doing something she never would have considered doing had she had been sober. Her husband caught her in the act and told her it was the final straw. He demanded a divorce. And now she sat crying, pleading over and over again: "If only I could turn the clock back *one day* . . . If only I could turn the clock back . . . If only I could turn the clock back . . ."

> "I don't need to turn the clock back one day, I need to go back to the day I was born!"

Guilt. Shame. Regret. Ever feel like that? One fellow told me, "I don't need to turn the clock back one day, I need to go back to the day I was born!" Some people actually feel that way, that all of life has been one big mistake. It may be because of things they've done, or because of things that have happened to them, but they wish they could turn back the clock.

Dealing with Past Sin

Many of us try to repress these feelings of guilt, shame, and regret. They're too painful to deal with. We stick them way down deep inside where we hope they will be forgotten. But down there they fester, and unless we deal with them, they will follow us until the day we die. Erwin Lutzer, of Moody Church in Chicago, writes in his book *How to Say No to a Stubborn Habit*: "You must deal with your past before you can experience freedom in the future. The sin that troubles you today sank its roots into your life yesterday. You can't break your sinful habits until you have a new beginning. Satan is particularly adept at using your past to ruin your future."

As I contemplated the consequences of divorce, I found myself saying along with the woman I'd counseled, "If I could only turn the clock back! If only. . . ." Now, however, I was at a place where I realized I had to go forward, not back. I could not allow the past to determine my future.

It is easy at this point to find someone else to blame, to absolve ourselves of our responsibility and attempt to free ourselves of guilt and regret. The woman I counseled who "fell off the wagon" blamed her husband because he wasn't sensitive to her needs. Some people blame their parents. Some blame their employers, the government, the police, their friends. When do we finally get to the place where we say, "I made a mistake"?

The Bible calls our mistakes "sin." Sin occurs because of the choices we make, because of the things we do, *and* because of the things we don't do. Sin is falling short of the mark. It is our inability to always hit the bulls-eye. It is failing to love the Lord our God with all our heart, our soul, and mind. The Bible says all of us have sinned: "For all have sinned and fall short of the glory of God"

(Romans 3:23). Even though some people will give you the impression this verse doesn't apply to them, it applies to all of us.

Lessons from King David

The one thing I wish I could have succeeded at in life, besides being a Christian, was to be the husband of one wife and have one committed relationship as long as I lived. But here I was, age thirty-nine, a fifteen-year relationship broken apart, soon to be divorced, a failure at one of the most important goals I'd set for myself in life.

Guilt? Truckloads full. Regrets? More than a few.

Despite my failure, my sin, I knew myself as a man after God's own heart, like our brother David. I find myself coming back to David again and again. He is so human, such a failure in so many ways, and yet ultimately a person after God's own heart.

The life story of David is outlined in the Bible from 1 Samuel 16:1 through 1 Kings 2:11. I tell people who feel defeated to reread the story of David. Most remember him as the author of the 23rd Psalm and as the boy who slew the giant from Garth—Goliath. There were many other giants in David's life, however, and a number of them defeated him.

David spent a good part of his life on the run, escaping from King Saul who, out of jealously and envy, wanted to kill him. Saul did not succeed and David became king, but he soon succumbed to lust and adultery with Bathsheba. In an attempt to cover his sin, he arranged for the death of Bathsheba's husband. Suddenly, David, "man after God's own heart," was a liar, adulterer, and murderer. Although he had reached the height of glory as king, he now walked through the valley of the shadow of death. His baby with Bathsheba died. His eldest living son, Absalom, sent him on the run again. Absalom attempted to dethrone him, and was eventually killed by Joab, the commander of David's army. When David heard of his son's death, he cried, "O my son Absalom! My son, my son Absalom! If only I had died instead of you—O Absalom, my son, my son!" (2 Sam. 18:33) David was well-acquainted with regret.

David's sins caused him much grief, guilt, and regret. Scriptures, especially some of the Psalms he wrote in the midst of his struggles, recount his difficulty sleeping and eating. The Psalms are filled with his laments.

David found a way to go beyond his guilt and regret and find new life.

David's story would be very tragic if it ended with his laments, if his final words were "I wish I wouldn't have...." But that is not the case. This lying, adulterous, murderer is an example for us. David found a way to go beyond his guilt and regret and find new life.

I became convinced God was able to give me a new life too. Listen to the new David in Psalm 32. He sings:

Blessed is he
whose transgressions are forgiven,
whose sins are covered.
Blessed is the man
whose sin the Lord does not count against him
and in whose spirit is no deceit (Psalm 32: 1-2).

The Living Bible paraphrases the end of the second verse this way: "What relief for those who have confessed their sins and God has cleared their record." I love that! A clean record! Many people feel, as David did, that they have a record. God has page after page recording all their violations of His law. Oh, for a clean record! Others have experienced God's forgiveness. They've had their records cleared; some, time and time again. Now they doubt whether God will clear their records again. Their guilt and regret are so great they become paralyzed.

Unresolved guilt and regret are very dangerous. Some doctors estimate that over 50 percent of physical illness is related to suppressed guilt and regret. Depression and other mental illnesses often result when guilt, like a cancer, eats away at one's soul. The guilt-ridden person is left feeling hopeless and worthless. *What's the use of trying? I've already blown it.* is the attitude many develop. Faith often evaporates. Satan, the master of deceit, has two subtle lies. Before we fail, he tells us that one failure doesn't matter much. After we fall, he tells us that it is hopeless—things can never be good again.

David is a good example of the consequence of guilt and regret. He tried to cover up his sin. As long as he did, guilt and regret ate away at the inside of him. He lost weight. His entire body ached. No matter how much he slept he was always tired. He learned to blame his problems on other things. After all, it was tough being a king and managing a kingdom, and he was at that age where men experience a "midlife crisis." But the cover-up no longer worked. David's real problem was sin and the shame he was trying to hide. Look at what he writes in verses 3-5 of Psalm 32 (TLB):

> There was a time when I couldn't admit what a sinner I was. But my dishonesty made me miserable and filled my days with frustration. All day and all night your heavy hand was on me. My strength evaporated like water on a sunny day.

David was at the end of his rope, but he didn't buy Satan's lies. So what did he do? Listen to his words:

> I finally admitted all my sins to you and stopped trying to hide them. I said to myself, "I will confess them to the Lord." And you forgave me! All my guilt is gone. Now I say that each believer should confess his sins to God when he is aware of them, while there is still time

to be forgiven. Judgment will not touch him if he does
(Psalm 32:5-6, TLB).

Many of the people I've counseled over the years would like
to believe that judgment will not touch them, but they can't. One
lady said to me, "I've confessed the same sin a thousand times, but
I'm not sure God has forgiven me." It is true that even though our
sins may be forgiven and forgotten there are still consequences.
David never got Absalom back. Absalom was dead. David would
never forget he had arranged for the murder of Uriah, Bathsheba's
first husband. In my situation, I'm still divorced and my children
live between two households. But think of this: we remember
David as Israel's greatest king, and the world most infamous adulterer, but God doesn't. God has no memory of David's sin. When
you confess your sin, God has no memory of your sin either.

God's Gracious, Complete Forgiveness

I heard a story years ago that so poignantly illustrates the totality of God's forgiveness.

An old monk asked for an appointment to see his bishop.
When the appointment was granted, the saintly old fellow
approached the bishop's desk and said, "Sir, I must report to you
that I have been having visions. In my visions Christ Himself
appears to me, and we are able to talk one on one just as you and
I are doing now." The monk paused for a moment before continuing, "He knows everything about me, Father, and yet His love for
me is beyond measure. Some of my brothers say I'm losing my
mind, but let me assure you I know the visions to be true."

The bishop examined the monk for a moment before he
replied, "You say you are able to ask Christ questions and He
knows all the answers?"

"That is most correct, sir."

"You say you have these visions frequently?"

"Almost every night, sir."

"I see," said the bishop, rubbing his beard. "The next time you have one of your visions where Christ appears to you, and you are able to ask him questions, ask him this: 'What was my bishop's chief sin before he was a bishop?'"

"I will do that," said the monk before leaving the bishop's office.

That night, alone in his cell, the old monk received a vision of Christ. He fell to his knees on the floor, although the love painted on Christ's face was not foreboding, but inviting. "Oh, most holy Christ," cried the monk, "My bishop has requested that of you I ask this question: 'What was his chief sin before he became a bishop?'"

> **"Tell your bishop, my child, that I don't remember. Neither my Father nor I remember his sin. It is forgiven and it is forgotten."**

The old monk expected to hear nothing notorious, but Christ's answer completely shocked him. "Tell your bishop, my child, that I don't remember. Neither my Father nor I remember his sin. It is forgiven and it is forgotten."

Dear reader, listen to the voice of God: "You are forgiven!" Read this account from Paul's letter to the Colossians:

> When you were dead in your sins and in the uncircumcision of your sinful nature, God made you alive with Christ. He forgave us all our sins, having canceled the written code, with its regulations, that was against us and that stood opposed to us; He took it away, nailing it to the cross. And having disarmed the powers and authorities, He made a public spectacle of them, triumphing over them by the cross (Colossians 2: 13-15).

You can have a clean record. Your list of sins has been nailed to the cross, and His blood has erased them from His memory forever!

After David confessed and humbled himself before God, he cried out "God forgave me, and my guilt is gone!" I can honestly say that mine is too. What about you, dear reader? If an honest examination of your life reveals unconfessed sins: lying, selfishness, self-centeredness, immorality, judgmentalism, or negativity, make a list of your sins one by one. Deal with each one individually. Make restitution, if necessary. **Accept God's promise of forgiveness for each of the sins, and remind yourself again and again that you now have a clean record!**

promise of forgiveness for each of the sins, and remind yourself again and again that you now have a clean record!

Now, rise up! Get beyond guilt! Live beyond regret! The best is yet to come!

Failed, But Not a Failure

King David accepted the fact that God had forgiven him of his sins of adultery and murder, but how could he move beyond the feeling he had of being a failure? It was a question I asked of myself. Whatever I had done to cause a breakdown in my marriage, I knew God had forgiven and forgotten. But I was left with this overwhelming sense of failure. The one thing I had wanted to succeed at, I failed at. It is this sense of failure that leads to further regret.

I made my memorable trip to the mailbox to receive my divorce papers in early February, but Tammy and I continued to share the same house for over a month and continued to go through some of our same routines as though nothing had changed. She told me she needed time to find another place to live. Every day she remained at home, I naturally gained hope she would never move out. She assured me, however, that she wasn't going to change her mind.

Failure at All Sides

During this uneasy time I dealt with a multitude of emotions: failure, fear, anger, guilt, and regret. Through the counseling I received from a Christian psychologist, I realized I had allowed pressures to control my life. Very much a "people pleaser" needing acceptance, I usually was most concerned about meeting everyone's expectations for me. When I failed to meet those expectations, I felt like a failure.

Along with the failure in my personal life, I experienced the greatest sense of failure because of my work in the ministry. In

61

the midst of my marriage struggle, one woman whom I had been counseling for years said to me, "I can't receive your counsel anymore because I see you are having problems of your own."

Yes, I'd fallen off the pedestal. I had failed. I had let everyone down. Pastors are supposed to be perfect. In agony over my failure, I sought out a well-known Christian psychologist, who, after a short evaluation of me, said, "You need to come to terms with your humanness. You don't walk on water."

> **"You need to come to terms with your humanness. You don't walk on water."**

But I had done about as good a job as anybody possibly could, trying to juggle all the things coming my way and keeping everyone happy. At least I thought I had. But as I had told many of my high school students, "If you are an apple, and someone doesn't like apples, and you try to become an orange to please that person, you will only be a second-rate orange, and you'll no longer be a good apple. Some people just don't like apples."

Listen to your own sermons, Guy!

You might not believe me when I tell you I can now look back at this time in my life and thank God for it. It wasn't an ending, it was a beginning. It wasn't a step backward, it was a step forward. It wasn't a death, but a new birth. Coming to terms with expectations, demands, pressures, and priorities was what I had long needed to do. It took a crisis like the breakdown of my marriage to finally move me to action.

But it didn't happen immediately—God is still working on me. Don't believe people who tell you they have reached the place they need to be. I still mix up priorities at times. I still fail at times. I'm not everything God wants me to be, but I'm pressing on.

Just like King David had to deal with his sense of failure, likewise I had to deal with mine. I have always loved the Psalms, but they took on new meaning for me during the period surrounding my divorce. I felt I was walking through *the valley of the shadow of death*. As I mentioned in the last chapter, knowing David had been there and had survived, and knowing God never gave up on him, gives me great assurance.

The Choice of Attitude

God showed me the divorce experience I was going through was the most important challenge and battle I had yet faced in my life. My doctor reminded me frequently that I could allow it to defeat me or allow it to send me on to new things. And what determined the outcome? Me. Me. I could choose to play the blame game, get angry, wallow in self-pity and resentment, fester with bitterness and regret, *OR* I could set my eyes on God and God alone, and begin recovery and experience a new birth.

> God showed me the divorce experience I was going through was the most important challenge and battle I had yet faced in my life.

The choice was up to me.

In my office I have a plaque that a friend gave me. It contains a Chuck Swindoll quotation that is one of my favorites. It reads:

> The longer I live, the more I realize the impact of attitude on life. Attitude, to me, is more important than facts. It is more important than the past, than education, than money, than circumstances, than failures, than successes, than what other people think or say or do. It is more important than appearance, giftedness, or skill. It will make or break a company . . . a church . . . a home. The remarkable thing is we have a choice every day regarding the attitude we will embrace for that day. We cannot change our past . . . we cannot change the fact that people will act in

a certain way. We cannot change the inevitable. The only thing we can do is play on the one string we have, and that is our attitude . . . I am convinced that life is 10 percent what happens to me and 90 percent how I react to it. And so it is with you . . . we are in charge of our attitudes.

I try to read that quotation at least once a day and remind myself to play the "one string I have"—my attitude.

Another story I keep coming back to again and again is a true story by Victor Frankl. A Jew, Frankl and many of his loved ones were arrested and thrown in Hitler's death camps at the start of World War II. Frankl watched and listened as hundreds of his fellow Jews were killed. He did not break. He realized there was one basic freedom no one could ever take from him. His captors could beat him, starve him, strip him naked, and they could kill him, but they could not take away his God-given right to decide his attitude. Frankl decided to love his captors. He decided to cling to life rather than give in to despair. He survived the death camp, and he is a testimony to the power of a positive attitude.

I learned a little poem years ago that sums it up quite well:

Two men looked through prison bars,
One saw mud, the other saw stars.

Or how about this great, well-worn story that well demonstrates the power of a positive attitude:

An octogenarian, widowed more than ten years, decided to marry again. He made a routine trip to his doctor. "Doc," he said, "I'm going to get married again!"

"Well, Jon, that's great news. Who is the lucky woman?"

"Well, Doc, she's twenty-five years old. And let me tell you, Doc, she is one beautiful girl!"

The doctor paused a moment before answering. "Jon, you're

over eighty years old. I don't want to spoil your happiness, but I think you should know these May-December weddings can often prove to be fatal."

Jon thought for a moment before he replied, "Well, Doc, if she dies, she dies!"

David's Example in Psalm 103

David understood attitude. He praised God in the midst of his struggles. Psalm 103 shows us how David got up and got going again.

> Praise the Lord, O my soul;
> all my inmost being,
> praise His holy name
> (Psalm 103: 1).

David could have blamed Bathsheba. He could have blamed Absalom. He could have blamed his biorhythm and he could have blamed God. Instead, he praised God and chose not to focus on his losses but rather on all of God's benefits.

> Praise the Lord, O my soul,
> and forget not all His benefits—
> who forgives all your sins
> and heals all your diseases,
> who redeems your life from the pit
> and crowns you with love and
> compassion,
> who satisfies your desires with good
> things
> so that your youth is renewed like
> the eagle's.
> The Lord works righteousness

and justice for all the oppressed.
He made known His ways to Moses,
His deeds to the people of Israel
(Psalm 103:3-7).

Look at the provisions of grace God gives us to overcome our
failure: He forgives us; He heals us; He ransoms us from hell; He
surrounds us with His loving kindness and tender mercies; He
renews our strength; He gives us justice when we've been treated
unjustly; and He reveals His will to us, just as He did to Moses and
the people of Israel.

What more can God do? The rest is up to us.

One thing I've found to be of utmost importance is to keep
reminding myself how much God continues to love me, despite my
failure. I think frequently about the old shoeshine man I wrote about
in chapter three. I've told many hurting people that story: "And Jesus
still loves me." David had to come to grips with this too.

The Lord is compassionate and
gracious,
slow to anger, abounding in love.
He will not always accuse,
nor will He harbor His anger forever;
He does not treat us as our sins
deserve
or repay us according to our
iniquities.
For as high as the heavens are above
the earth,
so great is His love for those who
fear Him;
as far as the east is from the west,
so far has He removed our
transgressions from us (Psalm 103: 8-12).

No Rejection by God

I've known many people whose failures have led to their being rejected. Some have been rejected by a spouse, some by parents, friends, and church. I know this rejection. When several churches discovered I was divorced, my speaking engagements there were canceled. In my local community I became the topic of gossip. I heard a dozen reasons why Tammy divorced me, none of them true. Some of the worst gossips were fellow brothers and sisters in Christ who should have been reaching out to me, but instead they seemed to glory in the fact I had fallen. Only one pastor in our entire area called me and offered me fellowship. I felt as though I had the plague.

This rejection hurt deeply, and I am still recovering from it, but I always remind myself to keep coming to God—warts and all—again and again and again and again if necessary. His response is always the same: *My love is available, My forgiveness always ready!*

I don't know what I would do without the Scriptures. Not only do I find great solace in the Psalms, but God uses His entire Word to remind me that I may have failed but I'm not a failure. Almost daily I remind myself of these verses, recorded by Paul:

> Therefore, there is now no condemnation for those who are in Christ Jesus, because through Christ Jesus the law of the Spirit of life set me free from the law of sin and death (Romans 8:1-2).

> I consider that our present sufferings are not worth comparing with the glory that will be revealed in us (Romans 8:18).

> And we know that in all things God works for the good of those who love Him, who have been called according to His purpose (Romans 8:28).

What, then, shall we say in response to this? If God is for us, who can be against us? (Romans 8:31)

Death itself cannot separate us from the love of God, and neither, I now add, can divorce.

Who shall separate us from the love of Christ? Shall trouble or hardship or persecution or famine or nakedness or danger or sword?

No, in all these things we are more than conquerors through Him who loved us. For I am convinced that neither death nor life, neither angels nor demons, neither the present nor the future, nor any powers, neither height nor depth, nor anything else in all creation, will be able to separate us from the love of God that is in Christ Jesus our Lord (Romans 8:35; 37-39).

Death itself cannot separate us from the love of God, and neither, I now add, can divorce.

And how far away does God remove our sins and failures from us? *As far as the east is from the west* (Psalm 103:12). Ever wonder why it doesn't say "as far as the north is from the south"? There is a north pole and a south pole, but there is no east pole and west pole. If you were headed east, you could never reach a place where suddenly you would be heading west; however, if you were heading north or south, you could reach a place where suddenly you would be going in the opposite direction. This Scripture verse wasn't written on a whim—it's God's way of reminding us again that our sins are remembered no more. A failure? Not in God's eyes.

Understanding God's Opinion of Us

It is important to understand why we are likely to fail at some time in our lives. I remember the psychologist telling me,

"You need to come to terms with your humanness. You don't walk on water." David writes about our humanness and why we are prone to fail.

> As a father has compassion on his
> children,
> so the Lord has compassion on those
> who fear Him;
> for He knows how we are formed,
> He remembers that we are dust.
> As for man, his days are like grass,
> he flourishes like a flower of the
> field;
> the wind blows over it and it is gone, and its place
> remembers it no more
> (Psalm 103:13-16).

In each of us there is a struggle going on between our two natures: a higher "new" nature of the Spirit, and a lower "sinful, old" nature of the flesh. As David writes, we are "dust"—or incomplete without God. God understands our humanness, just as a "father has compassion on his children." I understand my children's limitations. There are some things they can't do until "they grow up." Failure is often part of the learning process. How many times did my son Zachary fall down before he was able to balance and ride his bike? Life is like that, and no one understands that better than our Father.

Just as falling down is part of learning to ride a bicycle, through failure we grow and learn trust and obedience.

> But from everlasting to everlasting
> the Lord's love is with those who
> fear Him,
> and His righteousness with their
> children's children—

with those who keep His covenant
and remember to obey His
precepts (Psalm 103: 17-18).

God honors our covenant, our commitment with Him. His love is eternal, everlasting. This truth allows us to go on, even when we've failed. Remember God is God.

God is in control of your life and of the world. His opinion is the one that matters most.

The Lord has established His throne in
heaven,
and His kingdom rules over all.
Praise the Lord, you His angels,
you mighty ones who do His
bidding,
who obey His word.
Praise the Lord, all His heavenly hosts,
you His servants who do His will
(Psalm 103:19-21).

God is in control of your life and of the world. His opinion is the one that matters most. In His eyes you've been forgiven, your sins forgotten. He wants you to be His servant, to continue to carry out His will. You may fall, but God reaches out His hand and helps you to your feet again, and again.

So, dear friend, what is our response to Him? With David we can sing:

Praise the Lord, all His works
everywhere in His dominion.
Praise the Lord, O my soul
(Psalm 103:22).

Regrets turn to thanksgiving when we realize that God has taken our endings and made new beginnings.

No Fear!

Chapter Six

L uke, my son (not the doctor who wrote the book of Acts), has a *No Fear* sticker on his snowmobile helmet. I see these decals everywhere: on the backs of car windows, on the surface of skateboards, on the front of T-shirts, and on Luke's snowmobile helmet as he zooms past me on his Arctic Cat. I think it is a great motto to live by: *no fear*. Reality, however, shows me most of the world seems to function in fear.

Fearful of Going On

Once I accepted the fact God wasn't finished with me yet, and I was not a failure, I was confronted with the fear of going on. New beginnings are very frightening.

A recently divorced woman told me, "I look to the future and I am scared stiff! The thought of establishing new relationships, maybe dating again! Will I have enough money? How will my children adapt?" I understood. What's ahead, around the next bend?

> New beginnings are very frightening.

Fear is a universal emotion. It isn't exclusive to divorced people. A well-known pastor said that there are just two basic emotions: love and fear. There was a time I couldn't quite understand what he meant. Now I do.

Ann Landers receives an average of 10,000 letters each month, covering all kinds of concerns and problems. You've probably read her columns. Someone asked Landers if any one problem dominated the letters she receives. She answered: "The one problem above all others seems to be fear. People are afraid of losing their health, their wealth, their loved ones." She concludes: "People are afraid of life itself."

Regrets are like arrows that have found their target in our souls. We've been shot with them as we've run the race. We fear being wounded further. Fear will zap us of our strength and joy and lead to illness, real and imagined.

At a conference on psychosomatic illnesses, one internist expressed his opinion on fear and its consequences:

Fear of losing a job, of old age, of being exposed—sooner or later manifests itself as a clinical symptom. Sometimes this fear is nothing more than a superficial anxiety; sometimes it is so deep-seated the patient himself denies its existence and makes the round of doctor to doctor, taking injections, hormones, tranquilizers, and tonics in an endless search for relief.

Fear has two twin brothers: worry and anxiety. Dr. W.C. Alvarez of the famous Mayo Clinic in Rochester, Minnesota said: "Eighty percent of the stomach disorders that come to us are not organic, but functional. . . . Most of our ills are caused by worry, anxiety and fear."

Fear of further regrets will paralyze us. Like a battered ship that has survived a storm, we would just as soon stay safely in the harbor. This fear of further regret delights Satan because even though a ship in the harbor is safe, that isn't what ships are built for. As long as fear rules in our lives, we are rendered inactive, and we fail to maximize God's gifts to us and enjoy the abundance of a joyful life He has promised us. Jesus told us His will for our lives: "I have come that they may have life, and have it to the full" (John 10:10).

Satan delights when we become victims of fear because Satan is the instigator of all fear. Paul writes to Timothy: "For God did not give us a spirit of timidity [fear], but a spirit of power, of love and of self-discipline" (2 Timothy 1:7). Fear, you see, does not come from God.

Satan would like you and me to believe we are the only ones who experience fear, but the Bible teaches us otherwise. David knew great fear. This man who had bravely faced the giant, Goliath, was only human. What could be more frightening than being at war and being totally surrounded by the enemy who seeks to kill you? David found himself in this position. He writes:

Be merciful to me, O God, for men
hotly pursue me;
all day long they press their attack.
My slanderers pursue me all day long;
many are attacking me in their
pride (Psalm 56:1-2).

The Apostle Paul on Fear

The Apostle Paul also met the demons, fear and worry. It might surprise you that the man who told us to "live by faith" worried quite a bit. When we examine what he worried about, and what frightened him, we discover that they are the same things which worry and frighten us.

Acts 19-23 recounts, among other things, Paul's great work at Ephesus. He has just finished writing letters to the Corinthians, Galatians, and Romans. His third missionary journey now complete, he has spent over a year collecting an offering he now wishes to bring to the saints in Jerusalem. What could possibly keep him from delivering the offering?

Try fear.

As he prepared to deliver the collection to the saints, Luke records his thoughts:

And now, compelled by the Spirit, I am going to

Jerusalem, not knowing what will happen to me there. I only know that in every city the Holy Spirit warns me that prison and hardships are facing me (Acts 20: 22-23).

Paul didn't know what would happen to him in Jerusalem. He feared the future, the unknown, because Paul was human.

In his letter to the church in Corinth, Paul openly shares one of his worries and fears:

Now when I went to Troas to preach the gospel of Christ and found that the Lord had opened a door for me, I still had no peace of mind, because I did not find my brother Titus there. So I said good-bye to them and went on to Macedonia" (2 Corinthians 2:12-13).

Paul was worried because he could not find Titus, his frequent traveling companion and partner in ministry. Had Titus been arrested? Lost at sea? Killed? Paul went to Macedonia to look for Titus.

Paul didn't let fear paralyze him.

But notice how Paul describes his feelings during this time: "I still had no peace of mind." One version puts it this way: "I had no rest for my spirit." Paul arrived in Macedonia in search of Titus. See how he explains it: "For when we came into Macedonia, this body of ours had no rest, but we were harassed at every turn—conflicts on the outside, fears within" (2 Corinthians 7:5). In other words, Paul felt bombarded from the outside and torn apart from within. Can you identify?

Paul didn't let fear paralyze him. He found Titus in Macedonia. He delivered the offering to Jerusalem and went on to conduct the greatest revival of his career. He writes:

Rejoice in the Lord always. I will say it again:

Rejoice! Let your gentleness be evident to all. The Lord is near. Do not be anxious about anything, but in everything, by prayer and petition, with thanksgiving, present your requests to God. And the peace of God, which transcends all understanding, will guard your hearts and your minds in Christ Jesus (Philippians 4: 4-7).

Just think, God's peace will guard our minds and hearts, keep them free of paralyzing fear, worry, anxiety, and regret! We access this peace through direct communication with God in prayer.

Entrusting Fears to God

David understood the value, the utter necessity of calling on God for help: "Then my enemies will turn back when I call for help. By this I will know that God is for me" (Psalm 56:9).

Remember, God is for you, not against you! *No fear!* God is a most trustworthy parent. Our trust in Him acknowledges His love for us. If He loves us as much as I believe He does, of what do we have to fear?

The Lord is my light and my
salvation—
whom shall I fear?
The Lord is the stronghold of my
life—
of whom shall I be afraid?
When evil men advance against me
to devour my flesh,
when my enemies and my foes attack
me,
they will stumble and fall.
Though an army besiege me,
my heart will not fear;
though war break out against me,

even then will I be confident
(Psalm 27:1-3).

I wish my son, Luke, could live his life free of debilitating fear, but fear will come to us all and bring panic and pain. We have a choice, though. We can succumb, give in, give up, *or* we can bring our fears to God and entrust ourselves to His love and care.

We can succumb, give in, give up, *or* we can bring our fears to God and entrust ourselves to His love and care.

His love will conquer our fear. We have His promise. It might surprise you that the opposite of love is not hate, but rather fear. His Word tells us:

If anyone acknowledges Jesus is the Son of God, God lives in him and he in God. And so we know and rely on the love God has for us. God is love. Whoever lives in love lives in God, and God in him. In this way, love is made complete among us so we will have complete confidence on the day of judgment, because in this world we are like Him. There is no fear in love. But perfect love drives out fear, because fear has to do with punishment. The one who fears in not made perfect in love (1 John 4: 15-18).

As I look to the future, new beginnings, the fear of new regrets, just like David and Paul, I look to Him. If God is on my side, who can be against me?

I think I'll ask Luke if he can get me one of those *No Fear* stickers. I want to wear it on my chest.

And the Walls Came a Tumblin' Down

W ith the help of Christian counselors and friends, I slowly worked through the emotions of guilt, failure, and fear. And I continue to today.

A month passed after I had received the divorce papers. Tammy remained at home with the children and me, although she slept in a separate bedroom and communicated with me only concerning necessities. I maintained hope we would still be reconciled, although I continued to be met with her recurrent assurances it was over. Finally, a day arrived when divorce seemed more certain: Tammy decided to move out.

Moving Out Emotions

My son, Seth, has a most beautiful singing voice (all prejudice aside). One of his favorite singers is Michael W. Smith, and Seth has performed a number of Michael's songs in church. I heard Smith was going to be performing in Minneapolis, along with D.C. Talk, one of Seth and Luke's favorite Christian groups. I purchased some tickets and we made arrangements to attend the concert at the Target Center in downtown Minneapolis.

I called my sister, Janice, who lives in a suburb of Minneapolis, to see if she could watch Jessica and Zachary while Seth, Luke, and I went to the concert. She was more than happy to oblige, so I planned our trip to the Cities. I figured the concert would get over too late for us to drive all the way back to Brainerd, a good two-hour trip north, so I planned to surprise the kids and have us all stay over at a hotel, go swimming, and go to Camp Snoopy the following day. My children had been begging to go back to Camp Snoopy in the Mall of America in Bloomington, ever since we'd gone nine months earlier. I hadn't felt much like going to amusement parks, but having fun with my children brightens otherwise gloomy days.

I talked to Tammy about the arrangements, and she thought it sounded good. Then she hit me with the bombshell: "While you are in the Cities, I am going to move out." She explained to me about a house she had found and the location. She had made a month's deposit and arranged with the landlord to move in the first weekend in March. The house was located in Brainerd, less than two miles from the home we occupied together. We had agreed that the children would spend half the time with Tammy and half the time with me, and that we would work out a mutually agreeable schedule.

Although we had already gone through our possessions and agreed as to who got what, the fact that now there was a date established for Tammy to move out brought on a hundred new emotions. I literally begged like a baby for her to reconsider, but again she told me to quit punishing myself.

I think I was able to go through the process of dividing property because I still had not accepted it would really come to that. Now Tammy had named a date, and I found myself immobilized. I drove around town and did nothing but cry. I went to my friends Tom and Debbie's and did nothing but cry. I would go to bed at night and do nothing but cry. Amazingly, I fulfilled speaking commitments, but alone in hotel rooms and on airplanes and in airports I did nothing but cry. More than once a flight attendant knelt in the airplane aisle beside me and asked, "Are you all right, sir?" I would usually be quite honest and say, "I'm okay, but I'm going through a divorce." No one knew quite what to say.

I would arrive at speaking engagements, often at Christian events concerning the family, and I would face the standard questions: "How's your wife?" "Does your wife work outside the home?" "Why didn't you bring your wife?" I was not yet ready to open up to complete strangers concerning the depth of my pain and despair. The few times I did, it was as though I had announced a death, and people didn't know how to react. They had one impression of me, and I had just given them a picture totally contrary to what they had believed about me.

I didn't want to go anywhere, and I certainly did not feel like giving any speeches. This was my main source of income, however, and now I had agreed to pay Tammy a sum each month. The only way I could do that was to continue speaking.

I tried to eat, but my stomach was so upset that I lost all food. I spent nights kneeling beside the toilet at home and in hotel rooms. I had been bothered with stomach problems since childhood, but within a year after the divorce, it had become a serious problem that required major surgery at the Mayo Clinic. The sphincter muscle at the top of my stomach became so large and so used to being open it would no longer shut. Stomach acids raced up my esophagus through my throat all the way to my sinuses, leaving my esophagus raw and bleeding and my vocal chords damaged.

I tried all the pills my M.D. recommended. I watched what I ate. I raised the head of my bed. I ate whole bottles of Rolaids, Mylanta, Gaviscon, Tums. Nothing helped. I started to think maybe I would be better off dead.

Psychiatric Help?

My psychologist recommended I ask my M.D. to prescribe an antidepressant. My M.D. said he didn't feel confident enough prescribing antidepressants and referred me to a psychiatrist. I thought of all I'd read about the value of psychiatry as it concerns Christians. There was quite a debate. I knew a number of pastors who felt psychiatry to be a tool of Satan and scorned the thousands of Christians who turned to psychiatry for help. The real problem? Sin! Lack of faith! Not trusting Christ fully! It hurt to know some brothers would judge me "less of a Christian" if I sought psychiatric help.

When I was a teenager, George McGovern, Democratic presidential candidate, chose Senator Thomas Eagleton as his vice-presidential running mate. When it was revealed that Eagleton had sought psychiatric help, it cast aspersion on his candidacy and he withdrew, forcing McGovern to choose Sergeant Shriver instead. I have never forgotten that. So much stigma attached to Eagleton's seeing a psychiatrist that it derailed his entire candidacy! Although seeking psychiatric help has become commonplace over the last twenty-five years, to some Christians it is still an admission that one's life is not totally yielded to Christ.

I decided to forgo the visit to the psychiatrist for the time being. I realize now that I confused *Christ's sufficiency* with *self-sufficiency*.

A Weekend Away with the Kids

The weekend arrived when I was to take the kids to the Michael W. Smith concert and Camp Snoopy. And it was the weekend Tammy planned to move out. I still begged God that she would change her mind.

The kids and I left home after school on the first Friday in March. We made the two-hour-plus trip to Hopkins, where I dropped Jessica and Zachary off at my sister's. Seth, Luke, and I headed to the Target Center in downtown Minneapolis to see Smith and D.C. Talk.

While we were at the concert, Tammy and a friend were moving her into her new house. She had given me the address so I could drop the kids off there when we returned home on Saturday. Thankfully, the children seemed oblivious to how their lives would be forever changed.

At the concert we sat in the nosebleed section in seats where you needed binoculars to see the stage. Seth and Luke loved the concert, but mentally and emotionally, I was back in Brainerd trying to imagine what awaited me when I returned home.

After the concert, the boys and I picked up Zach and Jessica and went to the hotel so the kids could swim. I watched them splash and listened to them giggle. At times their volume was louder than D.C. Talk's rap. They kept urging me to join them in the pool, but I simply didn't have the energy.

Later, back in the room, I shared a bed with Jessica and Zach, the two smallest. "We can't forget to pray, Daddy," Zach said.

Should I pray out loud with them my most urgent prayer? I wondered. Zach prayed for blind people, so they might have enough money to buy a "blind dog." Despite my pain, I couldn't help but laugh uproariously inside. I pictured it: a blind dog leading a blind man. *Talk about the blind leading the blind.* But I knew what he meant, and I knew that God knew too. And I realized that God knew the real prayer of my heart without vocalizing it to the kids.

Seth prayed we'd "have a fun day at Camp Snoopy tomorrow"; Luke prayed we'd "have a fun day at Camp Snoopy tomorrow"; and Jessica prayed we'd "have a fun day at Camp Snoopy tomorrow." I thanked God for His great love, His constant presence, and for our family, which I asked Him to bless.

Tired from a long day and the exhilarating exercise in the pool, three of the kids were asleep before I finished praying. Ironically it was Zach who was still awake. I didn't realize he was awake until a few moments after I finished my prayer. Quietly his soft, tender little hand rested on my cheek, and he said "I really love you, Daddy."

I tried to hold back the tears. "Know something, Zach?" I asked.

"I'm the joy of your life?"

"How'd you guess?"

"'Cuz you tell me a million times!" He feigned annoyance, mixed with laughter.

Having never received what Gary Smalley and John Trent call *the Blessing* from my father, I've made it a number-one goal to give that Blessing to my children.

Soon Zachary joined his brother and sister in dreamland. I turned on the light and memorized them. "Oh, God, keep them safe. They deserve nothing but the best. Forgive me for anything I've done to hurt them—my lack of patience, my temper, my mixed-up priorities at times. Oh, God, forgive me." I was crying audibly now.

I couldn't imagine being at home without them there sharing it with me. I couldn't accept my family divided between two homes. I turned off the light and buried my head in the pillow. In his sleep, Zachary rolled over and put his hand on my chest.

Camp Snoopy

The kids were awake before I was to sleep, but they figured if they got up early they could get in a swim before we headed off to Camp Snoopy. Reluctantly, I climbed out of bed to go with them to the pool to be lifeguard, although they insisted they didn't need one.

Awake only a moment, I realized sometime during the night I had lost one of my contact lenses. I figured it must have floated away in my tears. One lens in, one missing, I asked the kids to join me as we searched the bed sheets for the transparent plastic lens about the size of a small fingerprint. Unfortunately, we were unable to find it, and even more unfortunate was the fact I had failed to bring along my glasses.

I knew it was going to be some day. I could only see out of one eye. I tried closing the eye without the lens, but it seemed so weird only seeing half of everything. When I tried to see normally my entire vision was unfocused, and I was quickly getting a headache. Eventually, I resolved that it was going to be a "bad vision day."

After swimming and breakfast the kids couldn't pile into the car fast enough to head to Camp Snoopy. "Can we go on the Log Chute, Dad?" "Can we ride the roller coaster?" "Can we get some souvenirs?"

I drove the five miles to the Mall of America with extra precaution. I should have put a sign on the ends and the sides of the Buick: "Caution: Blind Driver. Approach With Care."

At the Mall, one of Minnesota's wonders, the kids and I met my sister, Janice, her husband Jerry, and their son Michael. I appreciated the extra supervision, and the chance to spend some time with my sister and her family.

The Mall of America sits on the spot where Metropolitan Stadium used to. Only a few years earlier I had watched on television as the walls of Met Stadium were torn down. Met Stadium, as it was called, was home to the four-time Super Bowl contending Minnesota Vikings and the 1965 American League Pennant winning Minnesota Twins, who lost the World Series to the Los Angeles Dodgers. The Twins and Vikings were a big part of my childhood, and they continue to be an important part of my extended childhood.

Memories of Home Plate

As we all walked through Camp Snoopy, stopping periodically to ride the rides and view the sights, I couldn't help but think of the first time I attended a Twins game with my dad at Met Stadium. I wrote about it in my book *Molder of Dreams*. As I was reliving those thoughts, I glanced down at the floor, and there, embedded in the concrete of Camp Snoopy, was a bronzed home plate. I read the inscription with my one eye. It informed me the plate was set in the very same spot where home base at Metropolitan Stadium had stood.

"Kids," I yelled. "Come here! Look at this!"

They all came running. I think they thought I'd found a thousand dollar bill.

"What is it, Dad?"

"Look!" I said, pointing to the bronzed home plate. "Hall of famers Harmon Killebrew and Rod Carew stood here. Tony

Oliva stood here. Mickey Mantle stood here, right here!"

Seth and Luke, accustomed to my occasional fits of excitement which they usually didn't understand, seemed more interested in getting to the Log Chute. Jessica and Zach tried their best to appreciate my excitement.

"Did all those guys come to Camp Snoopy too, Dad?" asked Jessica.

"Honey!" I said incredulously. "They were famous baseball players who all played in Metropolitan Stadium, which used to be right here where the Mall of America is now. They all stood right here. Right here is where home plate used to be."

"Cool," Jessica said, as she ran off to join her older brothers who had caught up with their aunt and uncle and cousin. Zachary said "cool" too before he ran after Jessica.

I alone remained, standing at home plate awaiting the pitch from Sandy Koufax in the seventh game of the World Series. The bases loaded, two outs, and only a run behind in the bottom of ninth. I adjusted my ball cap with the red and blue letters T and C on the front. Proud to represent the Twin Cities of Minneapolis and Saint Paul, the State of Minnesota, and countless fans around the world, I prepared to ride a Koufax fastball over the big black wall in right center field.

Sandy reached down and grabbed the rosin bag and stepped off the mound. Tired of waiting for the pitch, I backed off the plate, adjusted my supporter, used my bat to knock the dirt out of my spikes, stepped back into the box, banged my bat three times on home plate as I crouched in my stance, and prepared to receive the 3-2 pitch.

Finally, Koufax delivered the ball. All the fans in Metropolitan Stadium were on their feet. Millions watching by television and listening on radio held their breath. The fastball shot toward the plate, knee high and on the inside corner.

Hit this one out, Guy, and win the World Series! Forever wear your ring with pride!

"Dad, are you coming, or what?" It was Jessica.

"Oh, uh. . . ." And suddenly I couldn't see the ball. My vision was out of focus. I only had one good eye.

I took a mighty swing that would have made Casey proud, but it did nothing but displace air.

"*Steeeeeeeeeeeeeeeeeeerike Three! You're outta there!*" The umpire seemed overly aggressive.

I stood dejected at the plate, tears welling up inside. The Dodgers mobbed Koufax, riding him on their shoulders. *They* would wear the rings. My teammates, Killebrew, Allison, Zoilo, and Tony were statues in the dugout, still in shock. They had come this far to have it end this way.

Oh yes, I would go down in history, not as a hero but as the one who had a chance but failed. There would be no ring for me.

"All right," I said. "Let's go ride Paul Bunyan's Log Chute!"

When I caught up with the group, Zach asked: "Are you crying, Dad?"

I made some comment about rubbing my eyes and trying to adjust to having only one contact lens.

Returning to a Home That Would Never Be the Same

I made the best of the day at Camp Snoopy, and by six o'clock even the kids admitted to fatigue. After a full day at the former site of Metropolitan Stadium, the kids and I bid the relatives good-bye and headed home to Brainerd.

I only had three hours left to live in denial.

I took the longer, more scenic way home, driving through the resort town of Garrison on Mille Lacs Lake. I told the kids I wanted to see the Blue Goose Inn, a famous restaurant on the banks of the 200-square-mile lake. Tammy and I had eaten many times at the Blue Goose and were having dinner there the night she went into labor with Jessica. Friday night, while the kids and I were at the hotel in Bloomington, I heard that the Blue Goose had been completely destroyed by fire.

The kids were all sleeping when I pulled over on the shoulder of the highway across from the Blue Goose. The yellow police ribbons surrounded a memory. Later it was revealed that an angry patron who had been asked to leave the bar portion of the landmark had doused the rear of the structure with gasoline and ignited it. While the Friday evening dinner crowd dined in the dining room, and the Friday night drinkers drank in the bar, the nearly century old logs burned rapidly. When the inferno was discovered, the Blue Goose was already engulfed in flames, and efforts to try to extinguish the fire were futile.

I sat a while in the car while the kids slept and other cars crept slowly past to join me in surveying the damage. *They'll tear it down. It will go the way of Metropolitan Stadium. They'll build another one, another Blue Goose, just like the Metropolitan Sports Commission built the Metrodome, but it will never be the same again. Ever.*

Smoke continued to slowly rise from the ashes.

One by one my kids began to awaken.

"Are we home?" Seth asked.

I knew home would never be the same again either, but I said: "Not yet, honey."

"What's that, Daddy?" Jessica asked.

"That was the Blue Goose Inn," I said.

"Why are you crying, Daddy?" Zachary asked.

I paused a moment before I answered, "I'm going to miss it."

The kids remained awake the twenty miles back to Brainerd, but instead of going to our house on Red Pine Circle, I took them to their mother's house not far from Brainerd's version of Central Park. I prayed constantly that God would give me the strength I needed. Thankfully, my tears were silent, and the darkness of the late winter sky was my shield. I played an *Adventures in Odyssey* tape for the kids, and it was finished by the time we pulled into Tammy's driveway.

Leaving the Kids at Tammy's New House

To say it was an awkward moment, an excruciatingly painful moment, the lowest moment in my life, does not begin to express the depth of my despair.

I could see the children were torn. They knew inside their mother's house were new bedrooms, new rooms to explore, and they loved their mother as much as they loved me. Both Tammy and I had tried our best to make it as easy as possible on the kids. The five of us sat in the driveway for a few moments. God intervened in a most miraculous way as I was finally able to say, "I bet your Mom is anxious to show you her new house. I bet she misses you too."

I let the kids go inside as I grabbed their bags and carried them to the door. Luke asked if I wanted to come see his new bedroom. Tammy and her friend stood behind him and helped reach for the bags.

"I've got to get home, honey," I said. "I've got to get ready for church in the morning."

I kissed and hugged all the kids one last time, and not wanting to prolong the pain and awkwardness, abruptly headed back to the Buick.

I thought I was prepared to go home. One of the elders from church had asked me to come to her house so she and another elder could accompany me home. They were concerned about what my reaction was going to be. I figured, however, I had to get used to being in the house alone, and the sooner the better. My stubborn Irish pride. My inability to admit I could use some help.

I pulled the Buick into the driveway and pressed the garage door opener. The door slowly opened. Even after everything I had just been through, I still half-expected to see the Dodge Caravan parked in its usual spot. *Stupid of me,* I thought.

I left my overnight bag in the car and quickly entered the house. Despite already agreeing to what Tammy would take,

I found myself gasping for breath. The house was nearly empty, no longer a home, but an empty shell, a sarcastic monument to better times. I went from room to room to room. Except for my office furniture, my bed, a broken recliner chair, and a table, the house was without furniture. Walls were bare. Cupboards and closets were empty.

A plaque remained on a bookcase next to the downstairs fireplace. It read: *"The Douds. Choose you this day whom you will serve. But as for me and my house, we will serve the Lord. Joshua 24:15."*

When my parents died, I grieved deeply. But this was worse than death. In death, love continues; but in divorce, love is expected to die.

I stood in the empty family room. "Oh God! God! God!" Each scream, louder and more intense.

My screams were lost in the sound of my fists punching holes in the Sheetrock of the family room wall.

Choosing to Rebuild

I punched holes in the wall, leaving scars on my hand and spots of blood on the wall. I actually foamed at the mouth as I repeatedly drove my fist through the painted Sheetrock. I was angry, very angry, and the volcano inside me was now erupting. Several years of trying to save my marriage; troubles in my local church; coming to terms with my workaholism, perfectionism, and impulsive nature; suffering from epilepsy, and going four years without a driver's license; debilitating rheumatoid arthritis; and a bleeding esophagus causing constant pain had left me questioning whether or not life was worth living.

Some Christian friends were quick to point out how we are to rejoice in suffering. Some of them reminded me of Job's friends, who all thought they knew why he was suffering so. They were ready with advice. Others told me to look on the bright side of things, think of all I had and how blessed I was. They all had good intentions, and much of what they said was good advice, but I wasn't sure that I could ever be truly happy again.

Accepting Psychiatric Advice

I finally decided to take the advice of my medical doctor and my Christian psychologist: I made an appointment with a psychiatrist. After an examination, the psychiatrist determined I was clinically depressed. I learned that clinical depression results from a depletion of certain chemicals in the brain. Chemicals, such as serotonin, become depleted through stress and numerous sad occurrences or losses. Once these chemicals are depleted, medication is usually necessary to restore them to normal levels. The doctor likened it to a diabetic who needs insulin because his or her body does not manufacture enough.

How could a Christian, a pastor, a leader, admit to depression?

Likewise, the clinically depressed person does not manufacture enough uptake inhibitors, like serotonin, and depression results. I later learned untreated depression is the number one cause of suicide.

I was depressed. Given the circumstances, it seemed permissible to admit it, although it still seemed incongruous to living the victorious Christian life. Didn't Christ say He had come to give us life, and life to the full? (John 10:10) Hadn't I been critical of Christians who lived lives of "quiet desperation"? How could a Christian, a pastor, a leader, admit to depression? Was it also an admission that my faith was weak, my relationship with Christ shaky? Was it an excuse to justify failure and sin? Hadn't I myself grown tired of counseling unhappy people whose lives always seemed to be full of despair?

Wasn't happiness a choice? Abe Lincoln once said, "Most people are about as happy as they choose to be." Was that really true? If it was, was I actually choosing to be depressed? Or was depression simply a chemical imbalance over which I had no control?

I had many questions, but one thing was certain: I needed help. Some people ask for help easily; others, whose god is independence, would rather die than ask help of anyone. My father used to always say that his favorite Bible verse was, "God helps those who help themselves." And for many years I believed that was biblical. It wasn't until I felt totally helpless that I learned the real truth: "God helps those who realize they are helpless." I remember the words of my recovering alcoholic friend who yelled: "I can't do it! God can! I'll let Him!"

Medication

The doctor suggested antidepressant medications to supplement the psychotherapy I was receiving.

I expressed my skepticism and apprehension. Even admitting apprehension seemed an admission of defeat, the failure of my staunch individualism. It is strange, being so independent, I have always so sought the approval of others. A paradox? Not really. Even independent people can desire approval for their independence.

On one hand, I feared what others would think if they knew I was taking antidepressant medications. On the other hand, I feared what the doctor would think if I didn't follow his advice. After sharing my fear with the doctor, he told me I didn't have to tell anyone that I was being treated for depression if I didn't want to, and he reiterated I should not feel ashamed. He went on to explain several different medications.

"Have you heard anything about Prozac?" He asked.

Indeed I had. I had read numerous articles about the drug. Some people called it a "miracle" drug, and some claimed it had caused them to commit murder.

"I've read quite a bit about it," I said. "And I have several friends I know who take it."

"What has been their experience? Do you know?"

"They have all mentioned it helps, but it severely affects their sexual arousal."

"Ah, yes," the doctor says, "that it usually does. Would that concern you?"

"Not being married, it is probably a good thing," I said, managing a smile.

"Would you be willing to try an antidepressant for several weeks? If it doesn't work, we can try something else or discontinue it."

"I guess I can give it a try," I said.

The doctor ended up prescribing Paxil, which is similar to Prozac and usually produces the same results.

Before beginning the medication, I shared my fears with an elder in our church who simply commented: "True love casts out fear. Jesus loves you and He wants you to get well. If this drug will help you, do you think Jesus would want you to take it?"

The answer was simple. Long ago I had learned that Jesus loved me and wanted nothing but the best for me. If this medication would help, Jesus would want me to take it. He created all the raw materials in the medication. He gifted the scientists who did the research to develop these drugs. He is, after all, the Greatest Physician.

Within three days of starting the medication, I noticed a significant change. Instead of waking up each morning with absolutely no energy and no desire to get out of bed, I awoke and felt a surge of energy. Given to extreme mood swings, I discovered life was leveling out. Small mishaps were no longer crises. I found myself more able to cope with circumstances that presented themselves.

Asking Jesus to Mend My Holes

My doctor was quick to point out that medication alone is not the answer. Medication can help restore needed chemicals in the brain, but what caused the chemicals to deplete in the first place? If I were to refill a gas tank that has a hole in it, what lasting effect would there be?

My doctor was quick to point out that medication alone is not the answer.

The doctor explained that one chooses to fix the hole in the punctured gas tank; likewise, one chooses to make the needed life changes to recover from depression. I was going to have to find the holes in my life and ask Jesus to mend them.

The knuckles on my right hand still witness to the night I punched holes in the family room wall. I could have left the holes in the wall, a witness to my angry passion, but I decided instead to rebuild, remodel, and begin again. It was a choice I made. It is a choice all of us can make when the holes in our lives have drained us of our happiness and joy. We can find the holes. And just as paint now covers the blood I left on the wall, Jesus' blood can cleanse away all of our guilt and shame and fill our hearts with hope to begin again.

The Enormous Decision to Rebuild

Choosing to rebuild is no small decision. Some people, so burdened by regret, fail to make any decision at all. The pain so numbs them they end up going through life in a trancelike state. Choosing to rebuild means choosing to make oneself vulnerable again, to risk failure again, to encounter even more pain. For many, the fear is too great.

I understand fear. For many months during and after our divorce, I withdrew and hid. I didn't want to get out of bed. I was always tired. Sleep was the only way to escape the pain, but it would come only in restless spurts, short moments interrupted by nightmares, waking to find myself alone in my king-sized bed. I would always get out of bed feeling unrested. Things I once enjoyed doing didn't interest me anymore. I would try to read a book and find it difficult to get past the first few pages. Life became a tedious chore.

Amazingly I was able to preach sermons—sermons my good friends told me had all the answers I needed. An earlier chapter in this book, "Failed, But Not a Failure!" is basically taken from a sermon I preached during this time. It is ironic that I could get up in front of several hundred people and say with seeming assurance: "You may have failed, but you're not a failure!" The truth was I felt like a failure.

My hometown paper contained a story some time ago about

a local business that burned to the ground, totally destroyed. The owner said he "was underinsured" and doubted he would build again.

If I were going to rebuild, as I knew I must, I would have to begin by checking the foundation to make sure it was sturdy.

I think that is the way it is for many of us. However, rather than being "underinsured" we are "underassured" and don't have enough "assurance" that it is worth it to try again. After all, are things really going to get any better?

Such is the result of accumulated regrets.

If I were going to rebuild, as I knew I must, I would have to begin by checking the foundation to make sure it was sturdy. A little paint can cover the blood, just as a false smile can hide the pain. But facades do not last, and ultimately, all masks must be removed. When the paint begins to peel, it is best to strip off the paint and get down to the bare wood.

Come to the Well

I f I wanted to rebuild, I was going to have to do more than just take a few pills each day. My doctor said: "Begin by telling yourself the truth."

Where to begin? If you want to see something clearly, it is essential to get a good perspective. A good vantage point is critical.

As I type these words, I am sitting in a hotel room looking out at Lake Superior. For eight years, sometimes several times a year, I have come to this hotel by the lake for extended stays to write. When I was struggling at home to write my first book, published by Focus on the Family, Dr. James Dobson mentioned he had to get away to write, finding it almost impossible to write at home. I took his advice and booked a three-week stay at a hotel in Duluth, Minnesota that has a beautiful view of Lake Superior and Duluth's Aerial Life bridge.

From my hotel room I have a good vantage point. I can see for miles. Docked in the harbor is the *William A. Irvin,* a large ore ship that has since retired and become a floating museum. On one of my stays, my children joined me the last day, and we toured the ship, amazed that something so large and heavy could float.

As I look out toward Canal Park, I can see many changes have taken place in eight years. Old warehouse buildings have been converted into shops and restaurants and new hotels have been built. Downtown Duluth has experienced a real renaissance.

The Vantage Point of Time and Experience

Many changes have occurred in my life, too, in the last eight years. When I first came here I had just been chosen the Teacher of the Year for the United States of America. I had met President Reagan in the Oval Office, and I was on the top of the mountain. I was happily married with three children, a new home, a new car. And I was the recipient of public admiration.

I first chose this hotel in Duluth where I sit now because it is the hotel where Tammy and I spent the first night of our honeymoon. We had been married in my home church in Staples, Minnesota on a Saturday night in June of 1980. After the wedding reception, we jumped in our car and headed for this hotel where we had a room reserved and dinner waiting in a revolving restaurant atop the hotel overlooking Lake Superior. We were told the restaurant closed at 10 P.M., and at 10 P.M. we were just pulling up in front of the hotel.

It was about three minutes after ten when we exited the elevator hand in hand and were met by the maître d' who looked at us and said: "Mr. and Mrs. Doud, I presume?"

We nodded. Amazed.

"Your table is waiting."

By the time we finished our meal we were alone in the restaurant high above the lake called Gitche Gumie, save of course the few employees who were closing up for the night. I remember the night as one of the best of my life.

Ah, the vantage point of time. Today I am looking in the same direction and at the same things I looked at fifteen years ago, but my, how they've changed.

Checking My Foundation

At one time I believed being a Christian meant things would always go my way. After years of depression, discouragement, bitterness, and anger, however, I came to believe the good times had all passed and the future would yield nothing but continued discontent. The last remaining hope seemed to be to think of heaven, and the mansion awaiting me there.

So why rebuild? Why invest any more energy into this world when such a better world awaits?

If I wanted to rebuild, and the choice was mine to make, I had to begin by checking the foundation and then assessing the current structure. What was worth saving? What should be thrown away?

As I worked with my doctor and support group, I found checking the foundation really meant taking a personal inventory. The inventory began with my belief system.

Some psychologist said: "You are what you think you are." The Bible says: "As a man thinks in his heart, so is he" (Proverbs 23:7, my paraphrase). So what did I think about:

God?
Starting over?
Myself?
My abilities?
My body?
My future?
My hope?
My ex-wife?
My children?

What I thought about these things made all the difference in the world. From the vantage point I have now, I realize that of the above list, the most important question is, "What do I think about God?"

One of my favorite preachers and teachers, Chuck Swindoll, wrote in his book *Growing Deep in the Christian Life:*

> I am convinced that there is nothing more important about us than what we think about God. Knowing

God shapes our moral and ethical standards; directly affects our response toward fortune, fame, power, and pleasure; gives us strength when we are tempted; keeps us faithful and courageous when we are outnumbered; enhances our worship and prompts our praise; determines our lifestyle and our philosophy; gives meaning and significance to our relationships; makes us sensitive and creates the desire for obedience; stimulates hope to go on, regardless; enables me to know what to reject and what to respect while I'm riveted to planet Earth; is the foundation upon which EVERYTHING rests!

I copied the quotation down years ago and have referred to it often. It means more and more to me each day. Sum up the quotation in one sentence, and it reads: "What I believe about God determines *everything* else!"

Unfortunately, many people seem so trapped by attitudes and behaviors they developed as children that they don't realize they can choose to change. It is much easier to say, "That's me. That's the way I am. I can't help it."

In his book, *Christian Child-Rearing and Personality Development,* well-respected Christian psychiatrist Paul D. Meier demonstrates that about 85 percent of our behavior patterns and attitudes are firmly established by age six. This doesn't mean, Dr. Meier explains, that people are forever unable to change their belief system. Of course not, but many people don't even realize they have a choice and choose to stay locked into those early childhood behavior patterns.

> **"What I believe about God determines *everything* else!"**

If change isn't possible, then life is bleak.

We come full circle to ask ourselves again: "What do I believe about God?" Does He really care? Does He even exist, or is He the adult version of Santa Claus and the Easter Bunny?

Using Faith to Change

For many people, a life crisis also becomes a crisis of faith. Will they *lose* their faith? Or will they *use* their faith? Consciously, I have never thought of giving up the faith, but to be quite honest, for many months I chose not to use my faith. I felt I had a host of legitimate reasons to wallow in self-pity.

> **Consciously, I have never thought of giving up the faith, but to be quite honest, for many months I chose not to use my faith.**

Faith is like love—the more you use or give away the more comes back to you. Choosing not to use faith is like having a seed to plant but not planting it. You don't lose the seed, but you don't use the seed either. You will grow no crop. The seed is really useless.

An unused seed is a useless seed. Choosing not to use the seed yields the same outcome as losing the seed. The choice becomes clear: use faith or lose it! Ultimately, I realized that the decision to choose was my decision. Others were willing to help, but the real changes had to begin with me.

I found myself back where I started. What do I believe about God? The answer would determine *everything*. Was hope possible? Could I go on? Could I love again? Could I risk again? Could I admit my weakness and confess my failure? Could life be good again?

God's Gift of More Faith

I didn't realize it during those dark nights of the soul, but even though I continued to confess Jesus with my mouth, I wasn't trusting Him with my heart. I had prayed so long and so hard that God would save my marriage. He didn't. After Tammy moved out, I prayed nights at a time that she would come back. She didn't. After the divorce became final, I prayed for a miracle that would bring her back. It never happened. Eventually, my prayers became less frequent, my study of God's Word sporadic.

During this time if you had approached and asked me what I believed about Jesus, I could still deliver what others called a "powerful testimony." I still clung to the faith I knew. I didn't realize that God didn't want me to cling to it, He wanted me to use it. And then He wanted to give me more.

> **I still clung to the faith I knew. I didn't realize that God didn't want me to cling to it, He wanted me to use it. And then He wanted to give me more.**

A story I heard as a child illustrates this concept well. An old prospector was traveling in the desert with a not-so-reliable map. Hot, weary, and out of water, he prayed he could reach the next watering hole before he and his mule both withered away.

At first he thought he saw a mirage, but on second sight he did see a sign sticking out of the desert sand. He rushed to it and quickly read: *"Old Well Out of Water. New Well, 2 Miles Due North."* Who had stuck this sign in the desert sand? And could the writer be trusted? His map indicated that he should head east, to the old well. Who to trust, his map or the sign?

At that moment he knew he faced a life-threatening decision. If he chose to follow the old map and the well was truly dry, he'd never make it back to try the new well. But how could he be sure that there was a new well? How could he trust some sign sticking out of the desert sand?

After much thought, he headed due north in hopes of finding the new well. Little did he know that an even more difficult decision awaited him two miles north.

The old prospector trudged on through the hot desert sand, his

mule protesting more adamantly. Finally, after what seemed forever, he saw something on the horizon that could be a well. His
pace quickened. His heart beat rapidly. Even the mule urgently
renewed his pace. Another quarter of a mile and there was, now
more precious than gold, a well, a source of water, of life itself.

Anxiously starting to pump the handle, the prospector
noticed another sign stuck in the dirt next to the well. It was written in the same handwriting as the sign two miles back. It read:

> *Well, partner, you've found the well. Good for you. But the
> well won't work unless you prime it.*

"Oh, no," cried the old prospector. "I don't have any water
to prime it!" But he read on:

> *A lot of folks get this far and they don't have any water
> left. I reckon you may be in the same boat. Well, don't worry
> none, 'cuz there is a quart of water underneath the rock ten
> paces to the left of this sign.*

The old man looked ten paces to his left. Sure enough, there
was a rock. He quickly ran to the stone and removed it, pulling
out a quart canteen of water. He was almost ready to take a big
swig when he remembered he needed to use the water to prime
the well. He went back to the sign and continued reading:

> *Don't drink any of the water in the canteen. Youse gonna
> need all of it to do the primin'. Dump the canteen full of water
> down the well, and then pump like crazy. You'll get all the water
> you need. When you're done taking care of yourself, refill the
> canteen and leave it under the rock for the next guy.*
> *Signed,*
> *Coyote Bill*

The old prospector thought the decision to head north rather than east was a big one, but now he had to decide whether or not to surrender what little water he had. Could he trust this Coyote Bill? Could he not trust Coyote Bill? What other choice did he have? Yes, he could drink the water in the canteen, but it wouldn't get him very far. He needed to replenish all of his water pouches, and his mule needed some water as well. What he had in the canteen really wouldn't do him or his mule any good, unless Coyote Bill was right. In order to completely be filled up again he needed to empty out what little he had left.

I don't remember where I heard that story, and I have probably changed it a bit, but the principles are all there, aren't they? I had reached a point where if I were to go on, I had to be willing to use, not just cling to my faith. Only then would I experience God's promise of new, stronger faith.

The old prospector had a big to decision to make, but actually it wasn't that difficult. What was the alternative? He had to risk losing what he could not keep to gain all.

I'm taking what faith I have, and I'm using it.

The preacher in me begs me to ask you straight out, dear reader, "What do you believe about God? I bet you have faced many challenges too. Perhaps your days have become even darker than mine were. You stand examining the foundation of your life, and you wonder whether or not to rebuild.

Ah, the vantage point of faith! I decided to go on. I'm taking what faith I have, and I'm using it. I'll have to pump like crazy, but I'll get all the water I need.

A Picture of God

Knowing that my behavior is directly related to my beliefs, I begin each day by confirming what I believe about God:

I know whom I have believed, and am convinced that

He is able to guard what I have entrusted to Him until that day (2 Timothy 1:12).

He is able, dear friend. He can. I'll let Him!

I close this chapter with a story from the Bible that illustrates most clearly how I picture God. Since we've been considering water and wells, this story is more than appropriate.

It was about noon when Jesus arrived at the Samaritan city of Sychar and stopped at the well, which was known as Jacob's well. Water was a precious commodity in Palestine, often more precious than gold. Although numerous natural springs were scattered throughout Palestine, wells were usually dug where no springs existed. Much work went into making a well, and they often became the center of conflict among people who needed water. Jacob's well was originally built by Jacob and served as a deep hole that collected rainwater and dew.

In those days it was the woman's job to collect water from the well, twice each day, morning and evening. Most wells, like Jacob's, were usually located outside the city walls, along a main road. The women would come, bringing their own waterpots and ropes, and would transport the water back to their dwellings. Since Jesus arrived at the well at noon, it was unlikely He would meet anyone there.

Jesus rested by the well, as His disciples went into town to buy food, but He was unable to draw any water from the well because He didn't have a bucket or a rope, and it was unlikely any woman would come to the well until evening. Soon after He arrived, however, another person did come to the well, a Samaritan woman who usually came at noon to avoid the other women. The topic of much gossip in the community, she was a sinful woman, an adulterer. Rather than confront cold stares and whispered comments, it was easier for her to come to the well when no one else was there.

Today she was not alone, however. Jesus was there.

It must have been an uncomfortable moment. One look at Jesus and the woman knew that He was a "pure Jew." His condemnation would be greater than that of her peers. No respectable Jew, especially a man, would even talk to a Samaritan woman. And if He knew the whole truth about her . . . well, thank God He was a stranger.

The Samaritan woman ignored Jesus and went to work lowering her rope and bucket deep below the ground. She heard the bucket splash against the water. The rope in her hand momentarily went limp before she jerked it, causing the bucket to fall to its side and begin to fill with water. As the bucket filled, the tension of the rope increased until she knew the bucket was full. Carefully she began to pull it to the surface.

I can imagine Jesus walking toward her, grabbing the rope and helping her pull it out of the well. I'm not sure that happened, but I bet it did. Regardless, once she had drawn the water, Jesus approached her and asked, "May I have a drink?"

The woman was shocked. How could He ask her for a drink? Even many of her own people would have nothing to do with her.

"You people usually will have nothing to do with us, what makes you so different that you are asking me for a drink?"

"If you knew who I was, you'd ask *Me* for a drink," Jesus replied.

You don't even have a bucket, or a rope, and this well is over two hundred feet deep! How can you draw any water for me?"

"I can give you water so that you will never be thirsty again."

The Samaritan woman considered that for a few moments. That would sure be nice. It got very tiring walking to this well each day and carting the water back to their dwelling.

"I'd love some of that water," she replied. "It is a long trip out here from the city and I get so tired having to do it each day. But how can You give me water?"

"I'll not only give water to You, but go get your husband and

I'll give him this water too."

"I don't have a husband," she replied, wanting now to change the subject.

"No, you don't," Jesus replied. "You told me the truth."

The woman must have wondered how Jesus knew this. Was He a prophet? Or had someone else in Sychar told Him about her?

"No, you don't have a husband," Jesus said. "You have had five husbands, and you are presently living with a man to whom you are not married."

Now she really wanted to change the subject. "Why do you Jews insist that everyone should worship in Jerusalem, when our ancestors worshipped here?"

"It doesn't matter *where* you worship. What matters is *if* you worship and *how* you worship."

Can you imagine how this woman felt by this time? "You must be a prophet," she said. "I am waiting for the Messiah to come and explain all these things I don't understand."

"Your Messiah *has* come," Jesus said. "I am the Messiah."

She knew He spoke the truth. She knew there was something different about Him from the moment He approached her and asked for a drink. He *was* the Messiah. He knew all about her and yet He still treated her with respect. Suddenly things began to make sense.

"I must go and tell the others!" The woman left her waterpot beside the well and ran back to Sychar. She didn't worry what others would think, but she went from household to household, proclaiming: "I've met the Messiah. He knows everything about my life and what I've done, but He tells me that even I can receive water that will bring me a whole new life."

You can imagine how skeptical the townspeople must have been. Yet they were curious too.

"Come meet this man, our Messiah! Come! Come!" And they did. For two days Jesus stayed at Jacob's well and ministered to those who came. Many turned to the woman they once had shunned as an adulterer. "What you say is true! He is the Messiah! He is the Savior of the world."

Jesus had made it plain to the woman at the well: salvation is for everyone.

The most important foundational building block is our view of God. Just like the wells we read about in this chapter, God is our well, our source of strength, of life itself. Sometimes we stray from the well and drink from other wells, but their water leaves us with continued thirst. My God is a well, who meets thirsty, hurting, struggling people, some who have abandoned hope, and offers them the water of life necessary to fill their empty souls.

Even those who have once been filled need filling again and again. And those who tell you they don't are lying.

Who hasn't heard someone say, "The church is full of hypocrites?" Someone said that to famed preacher Dwight L. Moody, and Moody answered: "Come join us, we always have room for one more."

Moody also said, "I need to be refilled again and again and again, because . . . *I leak*.

I leak too.

So do you.

Come to the well.

Come.

The Source of Much Regret

"Before you come back next week, write down five things you regret, or that trouble you. Bring the list with you and we'll talk about them."

"Only five?" I asked the psychologist, and we both laughed.

"We probably won't have time to discuss all five, but we want to begin sorting through the source of your pain."

I left the doctor's office with my assignment, figuring it really wouldn't be difficult to list five regrets, but as I was about to go out the door, the doctor added a kicker: "Try to identify the source of those regrets."

"Okay," I said. "No problem." The way I said "no problem" reminded me of the cruise Tammy and I had taken to Jamaica less than a year earlier. "No problem" were the buzz words of the island, and our cabin steward, a Jamaican native, would answer "No problem, Mon," whenever we asked him for something.

Here I was thinking about Tammy again, about our week-long Caribbean cruise, about happier days. Why was I having such a difficult time getting on with life, of living beyond regret?

My Regret List

At home I started working on my list. It wasn't as easy as I thought. Of course, at the top of the list I wrote:

Regret #1—Getting Divorced.

I had no more finished writing it than I was left with a host of questions.

117

★Of course I regret getting divorced, but *why* did it happen?

★What behaviors and circumstances led up to the divorce? That's what I really regret.

★I did everything possible to save my marriage, so should I regret something over which I had no control?

The word *control* struck a nerve. I had done much work with support groups and had led groups on codependency. I knew that much unhappiness in life is caused because people become frustrated with their inability to control all the circumstances in their personal kingdom.

Expectations That Produce Regrets

Every human being has a list of expectations. We have expectations for ourselves, expectations for others, and we even have expectations for God. We develop regrets when our expectations are not met. Sometimes we regret what we tried to do to meet our own expectation. Sometimes we regret what we didn't do to meet our own expectation. We regret what others did or didn't do to meet our expectations, and sometimes we regret what God did or didn't do as well.

When we hold such expectations, as most of us do to varying extremes, we allow circumstances over which we have no control to determine our happiness.

Let me illustrate with a true story.

I had been on the road for several days giving speeches and I was tired, lonely, and eager to get home. I pictured myself arriving at the local Crow Wing Airport and imagined Tammy waiting there with the kids to welcome me home. I'd come down the stairs of the plane and see my whole family standing there waving, Zachary, our youngest, in Tammy's arms, filled with excitement at watching Daddy land in a plane. I would reach the gate of the airport and receive hugs and kisses from everyone. Tammy would say: "It is sure good to have you home, honey."

The above is the ideal scenario I imagined. More realistically, I expected to drive from the airport and greet everyone at home. In reality, I landed, drove home, and found Tammy gone, and a baby-sitter with the kids, who were sleeping.

So much for my envisioned homecoming.

I must quickly point out here that I do not wish to make Tammy sound like the bad guy. She had every right to go to a movie with a friend. Countless times I had failed to be sensitive to her needs and meet up to her expectations. She claimed I always put my needs first, my expectations first, and failed to recognize her needs. She was largely right.

Two People, Two Sets of Needs

Two people look at the same situation and see two totally different pictures. How can that be? It is simple. Our perceptions are based on our needs, values, and attitudes. A quart canteen filled with water probably wouldn't mean much to you, but to the old prospector in the last chapter it was *the* most important thing in the world. Two totally different sets of needs determine two different perceptions.

A father keeps a misspelled, poorly written poem from his eight-year-old daughter tucked away in a book on the bookshelf. The poem will forever be a cherished possession. To someone else, the poem is nothing but worthless words scribbled on a piece of paper. Two totally different sets of values determine two different perceptions.

A husband is fit to be tied because the pastor's sermon extends for more than forty minutes and he is going to miss the start of the football game on television. His wife had been praying that the pastor would "put more meat" into his sermons, and she is delighted that the message includes tips for application.

Two totally different sets of attitudes determine two different perceptions.

How did I picture, or perceive life? Were my needs paramount? Were my expectations the ones everyone should heed?

Longing for Acceptance

As I conducted my personal inventory, I discovered that I felt pleased with my values and attitudes, but my needs? In my journal I wrote:

> My needs . . . What do I *need?* I have never lacked the essentials: food, water, clothing, and shelter. I have never felt underprivileged or poor. What I *have* felt is incredible loneliness. I have always felt left out, like I never fit in. I know that others love me, but it doesn't seem anyone loves me enough. Only my mother loved me enough, and she has been gone for almost twenty years. Her death left an empty void that no one else has filled. My sisters have tried to keep some of Mom's special loving traditions alive, but no one else has cared for me like my mom did. I always knew I had my mother's approval, no matter what.

As I go back now and read that journal entry, it is very clear to me: I could never have what I perceived to be my *needs* met. Nothing short of worldwide adulation and praise would fill the void. Jesus is God incarnate and look what people did to Him! Why did I have the need for such approval? One doctor called it "approval addiction."

I knew Jesus loved me despite my failures, but why then was it so important everyone else love me too?

The truth is my mother didn't approve of everything I did, but her love was unconditional. And hadn't I come to grips with the fact Jesus' love is unconditional too? Yes, I had. I knew Jesus loved me despite my failures, but why then was it so important everyone else love me too?

As I continued to work on my list of regrets, I started to see they were all related to my need for acceptance. I thought I had worked through this issue years ago, but telling myself the truth I realized for some reason I had a need to be number one. If there was to a best actor award, I had to win it. If there was to be a teacher of the year award, I had to receive it. I set my expectations of what I wanted to accomplish, and I was willing to do whatever it took to meet those expectations.

> **I truly cared about other people, but I didn't begin to care about anyone as much as I cared about me.**

No wonder I always felt left out. I was alienating myself from other people. I would be in a large cast in a play, often in the lead role, and yet I never felt a part of the cast. I realize now I felt that way because subconsciously I was letting everyone know that my needs came first.

Of course, some people saw me only as a very caring, giving, humble servant of the Lord. Why? Because it was important to be that person too. That is who I really wanted to be. I tried to give and give and give and give, and serve and serve and serve and serve. I tried to live by the Golden Rule, I thought. Now I realize that I expected others to do for me much more than I would ever do for them. I truly cared about other people, but I didn't begin to care about anyone as much as I cared about me.

It is very painful for me to admit this, but it is the truth. No sense rebuilding on a foundation severely cracked.

How did I end up feeling so entitled, so worthy of others' love? From the time I was a small child I had been "special." I missed most of second grade with rheumatic fever and juvenile rheumatoid arthritis. I did my school work at home. My mother waited on me and took care of all my needs. The doctor came to our house. I received much special attention. After a humiliating nine weeks in seventh grade Physical Education class, I got a doctor's exemption and never had to take Physical Education again.

The illness was real; the arthritis, crippling and painful. It also became a convenient excuse to use whenever I didn't want to do something. I got in the habit of expecting special consideration.

I wish I could tell you I'm totally cured of my selfish nature, but the truth is, I have to look to God each day and ask Him to crucify my pride.

My Real Regret List

As I looked at my list of regrets, I crossed out "getting a divorce" and wrote:

Regret #1— Living a self-centered, selfish, sinful life.

I didn't bother writing down four other regrets, I figured the one I had was the source from which all the others come.

What about you, dear friend? I asked one friend if he had any regrets. His answer was: "Yeah, I wish I hadn't invested in Japanese stock."

Maybe like Frank Sinatra your regrets are few, or maybe like my friend your regrets focus on really rather insignificant decisions you wish you had made differently. But if you are like me, your regrets might deal with major foundational issues in your life. As you realize this, you may gain insight into the circumstance of your life and wonder, as I did, how you could possibly have been so blind.

Whatever your circumstance, take it from one who has been there: it is worth the effort to rebuild. Discover the source of your regrets.

Courage to Admit Regrets

From years of ministry and counseling, I know that churches are filled with hurting people, but for some reason some people feel that they must "pretend" everything is going fine in their lives. Many, many times when couples have separated or filed for divorce, I have heard people in the church comment: "But I thought they were such a happy couple," or, "I didn't know they were having problems."

I remember one man who attended our church for several weeks. When opportunities came to testify, he was among the first to stand. When we had a prayer meeting, he prayed beautiful and insightful prayers. "What a tender man of God," someone said. Then several weeks later he was dead, the victim of a self-inflicted gunshot wound. Only later did I find out that he was renting a cabin in our area because his wife had left him and filed for divorce. And he had just been fired from his job. Why hadn't he shared his struggle?

> **Many people pretend to be somewhere spiritually where they are not.**

Many people pretend to be somewhere spiritually where they are not. One huge spiritual flaw is the belief that struggles are a sign of weakness and lack of faith. Another misconception is believing some people have no struggles and will look down on *you* if you do. True, some people like to give you that impression. And true, some people seem to be "holier than Thou." But the *real* truth? Read these truths again and again:

Everyone is a sinner.

No one ever reaches a state of sinless perfection in this life.

Everyone falls short of the glory of God.

No one has done anything to deserve sainthood, but

God bestows it to repentant believers.

Salvation is a gift made possible by God's grace through the shedding of Christ's blood.

There is none righteous, no not one!

The most righteous among us is still a miserable sinner, his righteousness but filthy rags.

The Power of Telling the Regretful Truth

Even many in positions of Christian leadership often bear very heavy burdens of regret. Pastors especially end of up feeling empty and thirsty. Unfortunately, they are often the last to seek help because to do so would be to admit vulnerability, and vulnerable people are often characterized as weak people. Some people are uncomfortable when you admit your faults and weaknesses. They'd rather you play a game and pretend to "have it all together." In some circles people *demand* you have it "all together."

I have discovered that by being vulnerable, I give others permission to be real as well.

After my book *Joy in the Journey* was published, I appeared on a well-known Christian television broadcast. My host had actually read the book, which I had written soon after Tammy told me she no longer loved me. I wrote the book while still clinging to the hope we could be reconciled. I shared many personal experiences in *Joy in the Journey,* and as she interviewed me, the host of the program cited several of the stories I had written. I admitted to my host that I still considered life a struggle much of the time, but nonetheless believed God could use suffering and struggles to bring us joy.

I had never been interviewed by someone who seemed so sincere, or who listened so intently to what I shared. As I continued to talk, tears flowed down my host's face, and she didn't try to mask them.

After the program was finished taping, my host grabbed my hand, and said: "You are so real. I feel as if everyone always expects me to be smiling and happy, and I can't admit my struggles and my pain. Thank you for being vulnerable," she said.

A few weeks later I heard this same woman was in the process of divorce and no longer worked for the ministry, or hosted the program on which I had appeared. For several years she had been the happy host, her struggles and pain hidden beneath the manufactured smile.

Truth That Brings Healing and Hope

I believe that God wants nothing but the truth. The truth can be very painful, but the pain is even worse if you continue to live a lie.

I have to admit that much of my pain resulted from trying to keep people from finding out I was soon to be a divorced man. I got up and spoke as though everything was sunny and rosy in my life. I told jokes and funny stories that made people laugh. I often condemned sin in such a way as to suggest I'd never committed one.

Soon after my divorce was final, I was asked to speak at a large and well-known church outside Los

> **The truth can be very painful, but the pain is even worse if you continue to live a lie.**

Angeles. I went completely prepared to project an image of the consummate saint. Before the evening service at which I was going to speak, I went out to dinner with several of the pastors from the church and their wives. We talked about all sorts of things, and then came this question: "Does you wife ever travel with you?"

My heart stopped. If I told them the truth, I figured they

probably wouldn't let me speak. I had been asked the question before and usually avoided a direct answer by saying something like: "Our kids are all quite young, and it is difficult to find anyone willing to watch them for more than a few hours at a time."

I justified my answer. After all, in my heart she was still my wife, and the four children were indeed our kids. This answer would get me off the hook. I wouldn't need to explain. I could avoid all the other questions that would follow.

It seemed as if hours passed. I looked around the table at these fellow servants of God. They were all real people, who had impressed me with their sincerity and honesty. I couldn't play the game any longer.

"I am recently divorced," I said, going on to explain the circumstances. Instead of the suspicion and condemnation I expected, loving arms went around me and many prayers were offered. Instead of telling me I was unfit to preach, the pastors encouraged me to share my struggle with those attending the service that evening.

Back at the church we met for more prayer, and when I finally stood to preach, the Holy Spirit completely took over. I shared my doubts, my fears, my tears, my sin, but my firm belief in God's love and matchless grace. When I was finished speaking, a pastor gave an altar call, and a large number of people came forward for prayer. I prayed with as many as I could. The pastors and other counselors prayed with the others. I watched amazed as crying people discovered healing hope.

The truth does bring healing and hope.

Regrets and Depression: An Inventory

I n the process of attempting to live beyond regret, I had already identified numerous issues in my life I was going to have to completely turn over to God. But one of the most difficult challenges I had yet to face was overcoming depression.

Large numbers of regrets often lead to depression. I'm not talking about just being sad. Everyone is sad periodically, but when you become depressed you seem paralyzed, unable to shake the gloom and

> **Large numbers of regrets often lead to depression.**

melancholy pall that covers your life. You don't believe it is possible to be happy again. You're stuck, wallowing in mud up to your neck.

I found it essential to determine the depth of my depression. I didn't realize just how depressed I was until I took a depression inventory.

I looked at the first set of statements on the inventory, which had been given to me by a fellow pastor.

1. Sadness

_____ I do not feel sad.

_____ I feel blue or sad.

_____ I am blue or sad all the time.

_____ I am so unhappy that it is quite painful.

_____ I am so unhappy that I can't stand it.

I checked the next to the last statement. I guess I had been able to stand it because I was still going on, but if much more came my way, I wasn't sure.

I read on.

2. Pessimism

_____I am not particularly pessimistic or discouraged about the future.

_____I feel discouraged about the future.

_____I feel that I have nothing to look forward to.

_____I feel that I won't ever get over my troubles.

_____I feel that the future is hopeless and that things cannot improve.

The directions for the inventory said to pick out only one statement in each group. As I read the statements concerning pessimism, I could honestly say that at varying times I had identified with each of the statements, sometimes within the course of a few hours. But what statement described the way I felt *most* of the time? There was no doubt I felt discouraged, and sometimes the future seemed bleak. But I knew someday, even if I had to wait for heaven, I would be completely whole. I would never give up hope, believing that things could improve.

During this time I was writing a book for a Christian friend. The book *Tragedy to Triumph* is the story of Reuel Nygard, a successful businessman whose twenty-three-year-old son committed suicide. Reuel's story of struggling to go on with life after such a tragedy was a real inspiration to me. Kelly, Reuel's son, was so inflicted with depression he gave up all hope and ended his life. One of Reuel's counselors told Reuel most people commit suicide because they feel they have exhausted all other alternatives. Reuel and his loved ones experienced much pain and depression of their own because of Kelly's death, but they never gave up.

I did consider quitting. If heaven is such a wonderful place, why wait? But God never let me follow this line of thinking very long. I would immediately think of Seth, Luke, Jessica, and Zachary. They need me. Yes, even though I am an imperfect father, they still need me. As discouraged as I became, I still knew I needed to keep pressing on.

Stop for one moment. Many people are discouraged. The regrets of life weigh them down. But do you know someone who is so discouraged he or she is ready to give up on life? If you know someone like this, you can't fix the problem, but do try to help. Be available. Invade your friend's space. Insist your family member get help. Tell the truth. If necessary, kidnap your spouse and take him or her to a doctor. Don't hide secrets. Fill everyone in. The person you are trying to help may reject you, even call the cops on you if you harass too much, but that is better than having a dead friend, brother, sister, or spouse.

> **Do you know someone who is so discouraged he or she is ready to give up on life?**

As I continued the depression inventory, I realized that if I hadn't had hope, I would probably be dead.

3. Sense of Failure

_____ I do not feel like a failure.

_____ I feel I have failed more than the average person.

_____ I feel I have accomplished very little that is worth-while.

_____ As I look back on my life, all I see is failure.

_____ I feel I am a complete failure as a person.

My deluded self was quick to point out all my accomplishments, but in my heart of hearts the man in the mirror was saying: "You blew it, Guy. Your family is broken up. You're unmarried and it is unlikely you'll ever be married again. You're getting fatter and fatter. You are a miserable, unhappy person. How can you live with yourself?"

God, that is the truth, I thought. *So many others see Guy as so successful, but Guy sees himself as almost a total failure.*

I must inject a word of truth here. No one is a total failure, although some people do picture themselves that way. Ironically, our society often pictures losers as winners. Was Howard Hughes a winner or a loser? He was one of the richest people in the world, but he died nearly alone, paranoid, and friendless. Was Elvis Presley a winner or a loser? He is still considered to be "the King," and fans perpetuate his myth. In truth he was a lonely, hurting man who died of heart failure caused by an overdose of drugs and physical abuse of his body.

At one time in his life Howard Hughes was considered the most successful man in the world. And at one time in his life, Elvis was the greatest recording star who ever lived. If you evaluate any life, you can find both failures and successes. The important thing to remember is that if you are reading this book right now, your life isn't over, and God has given you the freedom to determine your final outcome.

Even though I felt like a failure after my divorce, I realized that while I had failed, I was not a failure. Go back and reread chapter 5 which was written as a sermon about the time I was dealing with these feelings of failure. I can't help but think of the words of a friend: "You need to listen to your own sermons, Guy."

I'm starting to, dear friend.

4. Dissatisfaction

_____ I am not particularly dissatisfied.

_____ I feel bored most of the time.

_____ I don't enjoy things the way I used to.

_____ I don't get satisfaction out of anything anymore.

_____ I am dissatisfied with everything.

I quickly checked "I am dissatisfied with everything." That one was easy.

The next set of statements on the depression inventory concerned guilt. I had been able to accept the fact that God wasn't finished with me yet, but there were still deep-seated feelings of guilt, or was it really shame?

5. Guilt

_____ I don't feel particularly guilty.

_____ I feel bad or unworthy a good part of the time.

_____ I feel quite guilty.

_____ I feel bad or unworthy practically all the time now.

_____ I feel as though I am very bad or worthless.

As I read the statements about guilt, I struggled with them. I believe guilt is a good thing. Guilt results from sin. Guilt should lead to repentance, and true repentance to forgiveness. After forgiveness one should live as if he is forgiven, rather than continuing to punish himself as a miserable sinner. I had taken my guilt to the Cross. I had begged for God's forgiveness, but I was still overwhelmed with feelings—I wouldn't call them "guilt feelings"—but rather, feelings of shame. Even though I knew God had forgiven me, I couldn't forgive myself. The shame was too great. I may not be a failure. I am forgiven. But I am sure ashamed of what I've done.

> **Most of us realize that guilt is the logical consequence of sin, but shame is the badge we wear, like a scarlet letter on our chest.**

Shame is more difficult to overcome than guilt. Most of us realize that guilt is the logical consequence of sin, but shame is the badge we wear, like a scarlet letter on our chest. It is shame that causes much of what we can identify as depression. Read on.

6. Expectation of Punishment

_____ I don't feel I am being punished.

_____ I have a feeling that something bad may happen to me.

_____ I feel I am being punished or will be punished.

_____ I feel I deserve to be punished.

_____ I want to be punished.

Through counseling I realized that my shame extended way back to my early childhood. Not only did I feel that I deserved to be punished, but I wanted to be punished. As a child, I punished myself, by practicing self-flagellation. Such self-abuse is quite common today, especially among teenagers. Adults find more subtle ways of punishing themselves. Eating too much. Drinking too much. Smoking. Workaholism. These are but a few of the ways we punish ourselves. We do things we know are very bad for our bodies, the temple of the Holy Spirit, but we do them nevertheless.

When I punished myself as a child, actually beating myself, I remember hoping if I punished myself, others wouldn't have to. What had I done to deserve such punishment? I had failed to meet my own expectations. I wasn't perfect. No one knew that better than me. I deserved punishment!

These feelings of shame are not easy to recognize in a casual acquaintance, but when you get to know someone well, it is easy to see if he or she carries a load of shame. Lingering feelings of shame will lead to self-contempt.

7. Self-dislike

_____ I don't feel disappointed in myself.

_____ I am disappointed in myself.

_____ I dislike myself.

_____ I am disgusted with myself.

_____ I hate myself.

We usually think of hate as being the opposite of love. This is not the case. It is possible to love and hate at the same time. The opposite of love, remember, is fear. Consequently, it is possible to be so absorbed with yourself that you end up hating yourself for being so self-absorbed. For most of my life I had put my needs first, and now I hated myself for doing that. My doctor explained that this is a typical symptom of depression. Depressed people have a tendency to become preoccupied with themselves. By conducting an inventory with proper guidance, this self-preoccupation can be refocused.

8. Self-accusations

_____ I don't feel I am any worse than anybody else.
_____ I am critical of myself for my weaknesses and mistakes.
_____ I blame myself for my faults.
_____ I blame myself for everything bad that happens.

I knew that it was necessary to accept responsibility for my actions. Isn't that the same as blaming myself? Ah, the blame game . . .

9. Suicidal Ideas

_____ I don't have any thoughts of harming myself.
_____ I have thoughts of harming myself, but I wouldn't follow though.
_____ I feel I would be better off dead.
_____ I feel my family would be better off if I were dead.
_____ I have definite plans about committing suicide.
_____ I would kill myself if I could.

There is a common misbelief that people who talk about suicide never do it. Not true. Most people with suicidal tendencies give off signals. If you know someone well, you could probably come close to filling out this inventory for him or her. Not all people who talk about killing themselves attempt it, but the fact that they are talking about it is a red flag, signaling deep depression. There was no doubt in my mind I would be better off dead. I thought about various ways I could take my own life, but I never actually developed any definite plans.

10. Crying

_____ I don't cry any more than usual.

_____ I cry more now than I used to.

_____ I cry all the time now—I can't stop.

_____ I used to be able to cry, but now I can't.

I remember coming home as a child and sometimes finding my mother sitting at the kitchen table, crying. I would ask her what was wrong, and she would answer, "Nothing, dear, just give me a hug and kiss." I would willingly oblige, and my mother would brush away her tears and get up and start working in the kitchen as though nothing had happened.

As I grew older, I learned my mother was taking tranquilizers for anxiety. She often characterized herself as "a nervous wreck." She was always the most loving, giving, mother I believed a child could have, but I realize now she was very depressed. She often looked to her children as her main source of comfort. She needed us as much if not more than we needed her. The doctor says this is called "emotional incest." When a child feels responsible for a parent's happiness, it is a type of emotional incest and can be very damaging to a child.

> **One of my greatest challenges combating depression has been not using my children as my emotional support system.**

I grew up feeling as if I was never doing enough to make my mother happy although she always seemed to delight in anything I did for her. One of my greatest challenges combating depression has been not using my children as my emotional support system.

Resting in the Arms of Jesus

No one understands our tears better than Jesus. Sometimes when I come to Him in prayer, I picture myself a child in His arms. He is gently holding me, comforting me, wiping away my tears. No one understands like Jesus.

> **No one understands like Jesus.**

Taking a good inventory takes time. As I looked at the rest of the depression inventory, I realized I wasn't quite half-finished. I think I'll end this chapter here and encourage you to go back and look at the first ten items on the depression inventory. Have your regrets left you blue? Are you feeling depressed? Don't give up!

Picture this: Jesus is holding you in His arms. You look into eyes that are filled with compassion and understanding. There is forgiveness in His eyes. Feel His gentle touch. Know His tender peace.

Regrets and Depression: Further Inventory

I just reread what I've been writing. This is very personal stuff. Why am I exposing myself like this? There are a number of reasons. One reason is that I want to be understood. Another reason is that I expect I'm not the only one who is dealing with these issues. No, in fact, I know I'm not the only one. Recently I've seen billboards all over the State of Minnesota that read:

Untreated Depression: the number one cause of suicide.

According to the National Institute of Mental Health, perhaps 30 million people in America suffer from untreated depression. We know that 8 million are treated annually, and of those treated, almost .25 million require hospitalization.

> **In fact, Christians are often more prone to depression because they have a greater sense of failure in meeting expectations.**

Christians and Depression

Guess what? Christians are not exempt from depression. In fact, Christians are often more prone to depression because they have a greater sense of failure in meeting expectations.

I don't read my Bible like I should.

I don't attend church as regularly as I should.

141

The pastor preached on tithing again. I feel so bad because I've never come close to giving what I think God expects me to give.

The pastor keeps saying to witness and bring someone else to church, but I have a hard enough time getting myself to church.

They called me to teach Sunday School, but I just couldn't make that commitment. Besides, I don't think I'd be a very good teacher anyhow. I don't know much.

I could write an entire book of statements made by Christians who feel they have failed to "measure up." Take a moment right now and write down a few of your own "failure statements." How have you failed to measure up?

I've got news for you, friend: everyone fails to measure up to God! If we did measure up, we wouldn't need a Savior, would we?

Choosing Self-condemnation or God's Forgiveness

As I continue to live beyond the regret and the depression resulting from unmet expectations, I've learned that changing my "self-talk" is essential. I can *choose* to condemn myself as a failure, or I can *choose* to accept God's forgiveness and grace. My attitude changes what I tell myself in my head.

I can choose to condemn myself as a failure, or I can choose to accept God's forgiveness and grace.

Instead of saying: "Guy, you are a failure!" I can choose to say: "Guy, God wants you to put the past behind you and get up and get going on! You've been forgiven. Your sins have been forgotten. So live like a believer! You're redeemed! Live like it!"

Why had I chosen to listen to all the negative self-talk? Why do so many of us listen to the negative self-talk? I believe it stems from regrets, guilt, and shame, which all lead us to conclude we deserve to be punished. Well, we do deserve to be punished, but Jesus was punished in our place. When we punish ourselves, in a real sense, we are rejecting Christ's gift of grace.

A pastor friend said: "You can punish yourself all you want, but it cannot atone for your sin. So what purpose does punishment serve? Does it satisfy some misguided notion you're getting what you deserve? Hey, you still have to suffer the consequences of your sins, but Jesus paid the penalty."

It was time to continue my inventory. In the last chapter I shared personal evaluations of each list and how I was feeling at the time. I did this to provide an example to you of how you can take a similar inventory. Although I will expound on a few of the following items, I'm not going to go into detail on each one. Nevertheless, I hope you take the time you need to conduct your inventory.

11. Irritability

_____ I am no more irritated now than I ever am.

_____ I get annoyed or irritated more easily than I used to.

_____ I feel irritated all the time.

_____ I don't get irritated at all at things that used to irritate me.

Notice the progression of statements under irritability. They are very similar to the statements on crying, stated in the last chapter. In the crying list, the last two statements go from *crying all the time* to *never crying at all*. In the irritability list, the last two statements go from *feeling irritated all the time* to *not being irritated at all*.

What happens when you reach the final depths of depression is that you become so numb and so paralyzed you no longer care. Hence, tears don't come and irritability doesn't surface because you have no feelings left.

And a person with no feelings left often experiences alienation.

12. Social Withdrawal

_____ I have not lost interest in other people.

_____ I am less interested in other people than I used to be.

_____ I have lost most of my interest in other people and have little feeling for them.

_____ I have lost all my interest in other people.

I've already explained that most depressed people are preoccupied with themselves. This preoccupation becomes more and more severe as depression deepens. Eventually, depressed people have no interest in anything other than themselves. I've confessed to being self-absorbed. It sounds harsh, but my depression, and perhaps many others' depression, is really a grand form of selfishness.

This is why many doctors encourage depressed people to find someone else to reach out to. It is similar with lonely people. Many lonely people long for relationships and for someone to call them and invite them to be included. What would happen, however, if everyone sat around waiting to be called and included? In a real sense, loneliness is another form of selfishness. The old adage is true: If you want to have friends, be a friend.

Unfortunately, some people's depression becomes so deep they need outside help to get them going again. Anti-depressant medications and cognitive therapy are highly successful in treating depression. With proper guidance, the depressed person is able to become well again.

13. Body Image Changes

_____ I don't feel I look any worse than I used to.

_____ I am worried that I am looking old or unattractive.

_____ I feel that there are permanent changes in my appetite, and they make me unattractive.

_____ I feel that I am ugly or repulsive looking.

When I became National Teacher of the Year in 1986, I

weighed 170 pounds. When I graduated from college in 1975, I weighed 330 pounds. In *Molder of Dreams* I explain how I went about losing the weight, confessing that I forced myself to regurgitate after eating, fearing that I would gain all my weight back. This became a bad habit.

I had received so many compliments on the "new me" that I could never imagine myself becoming overly obese again. I gave all my "fat" clothes to the Salvation Army and bought a whole new wardrobe. It was exciting going from a 54" waist to a 32" waist. I was thrilled to replace 22" neck shirts with shirts with a 16" collar. Even the size of my shoe decreased from a 12 to a 10 1/2.

It was essential to my self-image that I stay "skinny" so I continued to be bulimic. Tammy would fix a great meal. I would eat heartily, then go into the bathroom and force myself to vomit. Tammy expected it, confronted me, and I denied it. Finally, she quit confronting me. I think most of my close friends knew I frequently forced myself to regurgitate, but only one ever confronted me. I lied to my friend too.

> **Here I was writing Christian books, making videos, pastoring a church, and lying.**

Perhaps by sharing this, you can see how it is possible to come to hate yourself for being such a hypocrite. Here I was writing Christian books, making videos, pastoring a church, and lying. Lie enough and your whole life becomes a lie. You become so angry at yourself, and you don't know what to do with the anger. You keep it inside and your depression worsens. Every aspect of your life is affected.

14. Work Retardation

_____ I can work about as well as before.

_____ It takes extra effort to get started at doing something.

_____ I don't work as well as I used to.
_____ I have to push myself very hard to do anything.
_____ I can't do my work at all.

15. Insomnia

_____ I can sleep as well as usual.
_____ I wake up more tired in the morning than I used to.
_____ I wake up to one or two hours earlier than usual and find it hard to get back to sleep.
_____ I wake up early every day and can't get more than five hours of sleep.

16. Fatigue

_____ I don't get any more tired than usual.
_____ I get tired more easily than I used to.
_____ I get tired from doing anything.
_____ I get too tired to do anything.

17. Anorexia

_____ My appetite is no worse than usual.
_____ My appetite is not as good as it used to be.
_____ My appetite is much worse now.
_____ I have no appetite at all anymore.

18. Weight Loss

_____ I haven't lost much weight, if any, lately.
_____ I have lost more than five pounds.
_____ I have lost more than ten pounds.
_____ I have lost more than twenty pounds.

19. Health

_____ I am no more concerned about my health than usual.
_____ I am concerned about aches and pains or upset stomach or constipation.

_____ I am so concerned with how I feel or what I feel that it's hard to think of anything else.

_____ I am completely absorbed in what I feel and am unable to think of much else.

20. Indecisiveness

_____ I make decisions about as well as ever.

_____ I try to put off making decisions.

_____ I have great difficulty making decisions.

_____ I can't make any decisions anymore.

21. Sex Drive

_____ I have not noticed any recent change in interest in sex.

_____ I am less interested in sex than I used to be.

_____ I am much less interested in sex now.

_____ I have lost interest in sex completely.

The Effects of Depression on My Body

When I decided to face my depression head on, I realized that I had to start taking care of my body. It was almost too late. Although I had quit forcing myself to vomit, the damage was already done. The sphincter muscle at the top of my stomach had become so large that food would no longer stay in my stomach. Consequently, the food and acids in my stomach forced their way up my esophagus and into my sinuses. I would wake at night choking on the food and acid in my mouth.

I saw a picture taken by a scope at the Mayo Clinic in Rochester, Minnesota. It showed my esophagus, raw and bleeding. It also showed a large hiatal hernia protruding between my lungs.

A thorough examination at the Clinic revealed other health problems as well, most notably, severe sleep apnea. During an evaluation at the Mayo's Sleep Disorder Clinic, I stopped breathing eighty-seven times in ninety minutes. I would wake up, gasp for breath, go back to sleep, and wake up again. The tissues in the back of my throat were preventing the air from going to the lungs, causing a cessation of breathing. The volume of my snoring ranked a "four" on the Mayo chart, the equivalent of a jet plane taking off. I was a champion snorer!

One time while I was staying at a hotel in Grand Rapids, Michigan, the front desk called me three times to ask me to turn down my stereo. It was the middle of the night, and I wasn't listening to music. I was asleep. When the security guard came to my door, he was able to figure out that my snoring had been mistaken for bass sound coming from a boom box!

People who suffer from sleep apnea usually get up in the morning feeling unrested. In addition, they are more susceptible to high blood pressure and heart attacks. Since they usually feel fatigued, exercise is difficult, so they often become more obese, making the apnea even worse. I had been hospitalized and in intensive care a number of times with suspected heart attacks, but thankfully the episodes weren't heart attacks, but chest pains caused by stress and anxiety.

It is no secret that emotional pain often leads to real physical pain, and emotional illness to physical illness.

During the evaluation at the Mayo Clinic, the MMPI (Minnesota Multi-Phasic Inventory) test indicated I was—you guessed it—depressed, and I discussed my course of treatment with my doctor.

It is no secret that emotional pain often leads to real physical pain, and emotional illness to physical illness. In addition to the hernia, apnea, and depression, my rheumatoid arthritis, in remission since college days, became active again, inflicting most of the joints in my body.

I discussed my situation with my doctors at Mayo. They said: "Let's tackle one thing at a time. The most pressing problem is your stomach. You need surgery."

The surgeon recommended I undergo what he called a Belsy procedure. He would cut from near my spine on my back, under my right arm pit, through a rib or two, pull out part of my stomach, take part of the esophagus, wrap it 180 degrees around the top of my stomach, and make a new sphincter muscle. He would then take the protruding part of my stomach and shove it back down where it was supposed to be and fix my diaphragm to hold it in place.

The doctor explained it was an extensive surgery and my recovery would include at least ten days in the hospital and at least three months of limited activity. My ribs would still hurt for about a year, and it was likely my bowels would take a while to adjust. The up side was I would have no more heartburn and no more bleeding.

Although I found decisions increasingly difficult to make, I felt I really didn't have any choice concerning the surgery. I needed it. Reluctantly, I scheduled the surgery, not knowing how I would be able to take care of myself and my four children while I recuperated. I was forced to trust God for this one. I didn't like the feeling of not being in control.

Never All Alone

A s the day approached for my upcoming surgery, several things became crystal clear: one, regrets gave way to anxiety and fear; two, I realized I wanted to live; and three, I suddenly felt all alone.

In a strange way, anxiety isn't as debilitating as regret. With anxiety, there is always the possibility things will turn out better than expected, but with regret things have already happened and been deemed failures. At least there was a good chance the surgery would improve my overall health and well-being.

Once again, I heard God say: "Get in the wheelbarrow, Guy! Use the little water you have to prime the pump!"

The Surgeon's Instructions

The surgery was scheduled for a Wednesday at 6:30 in the morning. It just happened to be Ash Wednesday, the beginning of Lent.

"Nothing by mouth after midnight Tuesday," the surgeon instructed. "I will meet with you and your wife prior to the surgery, and I will keep your family updated as to your progress throughout the surgery. I'll probably stop halfway through the surgery and let them know how it's going."

"I don't have a wife, and I don't think anyone from my family will be present," I admitted. "I'm divorced, and my four children are all ten or under, so they won't be able to come."

I saw the surgeon's eyes glance at my left hand—he had seen a wedding ring—and then he glanced at my chart.

"Well, who is going to be home to take care of you when

153

you are released from the hospital? You're not going to feel like doing anything for at least six weeks."

"I have lots of friends," I said. "And people from my church have volunteered to take turns making dinner for us and cleaning the house."

"Well, who is going to be home to take care of you when you are released from the hospital?"

"You shouldn't be alone for a while," the doctor continued. "Maybe you should consider going into a nursing home for a few weeks."

The thought shocked me. A nursing home? I had definite feelings about nursing homes. Even the best ones depressed me. I remembered one experience at a nursing home. As a Boy Scout, we were Christmas caroling at the local nursing home when one of the residents, an elderly lady, began yelling at us: "You come here at Christmas and think we should appreciate your good deeds, but you forget about us the rest of the year. I'd rather you not come at all!" Her outburst shocked me.

My dad had always made us promise we wouldn't put him in a nursing home, and he seemed very serious. And I had a friend whose grandmother had refused to go into a nursing home, but she was finally forced to. The first night in the home she died; her heart just stopped beating. My friend said, "I think Grandma died of a broken heart."

Being a pastor, I knew hospitals were under pressure to move patients out quickly. I knew that many people went to nursing homes until they were able to take care of themselves once again at home. Usually, these patients were single or had a spouse who was unable to care for them. The reality hit me: I had no one person to whom I could turn for constant support and care. My mother had always filled that role in my life when she was alive, and Tammy had been my helpmate while we were married. But now, no mom, no wife, no children, no siblings were able to provide constant care, and I faced the prospect of going into a nursing home. I never felt more alone.

"I'm sure I won't need to go into a nursing home," I told the doctor, convincing myself.

"Well, it is an option."

"I'm sure I'll be just fine."

"Will there be anyone here with you during the surgery?" the doctor questioned.

"I don't think so. Everyone I know lives too far away."

"We don't expect any problems with your surgery, but it is nice to have someone there with you when you wake up."

"I'll be fine."

"All right," the doctor said. "If you don't have any more questions, I'll have my assistant explain a few more details to you and I'll see you Wednesday."

Feeling Utterly Alone

Recently, a man from New York State called my office and told my secretary he had to speak to me. I phoned him back later the same day, not knowing what to expect. I reached the man, named Vern, and found him almost unable to speak. He explained he had emphysema and it was difficult for him to breathe because he had almost no lung capacity left. "I'm not long for this world," he said with obvious regret in his voice.

"I've never been a religious man, " he continued, "but I saw your film *Molder of Dreams,* and it really touched me. I just wanted to talk to you."

"I'm not very religious either," I said.

"You sure sound religious in the movie." It took some effort for him to get the sentence out.

"I guess it has to do with what you mean by *religious.* I think of my faith as a relationship, a friendship with Jesus, not something I practice to earn me favor."

"Well, I was raised where I had to go to mass every week, and confession, and say the rosary, and do penance, and I never thought of Jesus being my friend."

"You can't find a better friend," I encouraged him.

Although it was difficult for him to speak, we continued talking for over an hour. He fired question after question at me concerning God and Jesus and the Holy Spirit. Finally, he asked: "Why did Jesus yell out on the Cross that God had deserted Him?"

"Have you ever felt lonely?" I asked, slowly.

"Yeah, I'm lonely right now. My wife and I haven't had an intimate relationship in over eighteen years, and my two kids never come home, 'cuz I guess I was too hard on them when they were growing up."

There was a long pause as he summoned up enough breath: "God, I'm lonely. . . ." And he began to sob.

"Jesus understands loneliness, Vern. No one has ever felt lonelier than He did when He hung on the cross between two thieves, a willing sacrifice for all the sins of humankind. In His humanness He cried out: 'My God, My God, why have You forsaken Me?' Jesus understood what it felt like to be all alone."

There was silence on the phone. I was worried I had sounded too much like a pastor. Finally, a question came from Vern: "Have you ever felt real lonely, Mr. Doud?"

His question immediately produced an image in my mind. I saw myself on a cart being wheeled into a cold, sterile room where I was prepped for surgery. I said my good-byes to three friends who had spent the night with me prior to surgery, knowing they were unable to stay with me while the surgery took place. I knew when I came out of surgery, *if I did,* I'd be alone. And as the nurse began to shave the hair off my chest, I felt totally isolated from the rest of the world.

Jesus understood what it felt like to be all alone.

"You sure have a lot of hair on your chest," the male nurse said.

"Yeah," I answered, and then, always the jokester, added: "When I was a kid my dad always told me to eat my vegetables because it would put hair on my chest. I never wanted hair on my chest, so I never ate my vegetables. And look at me."

The nurse laughed, but I was thinking of my dad, my mom, my wife, ah, my ex-wife. . . .

"My chest is going to itch like crazy as all the hair grows back. I'll remember you, sir. I'll remember you."

The nurse laughed again.

He finished shaving my chest, exhausting at least two disposable razors, and then he said, "I'm going to have to take your glasses, and your watch, and, let's see, do you have any other jewelry?"

"Here, take this too," I said, removing the wedding ring from my left hand.

"These items will be returned to you after your surgery. Your surgery should go fine. They'll come get you in a few minutes and take you into surgery. Take care." And he was gone.

"Thanks," I said, but he was already gone, and I lay staring at the ceiling. At least I was looking up.

Jesus, Jesus, Jesus

I stared upward for a long time before I prayed: "Okay, God. It's just You and me. I know You're with me. I'm not alone."

Another nurse gave me a shot to relax, and I hardly remember being taken into the operating room, except that it was very cold, and they put warm blankets on me that felt very good.

When I awoke, nearly twelve hours later, I was in a haze unlike anything I had ever experienced. Initially, I panicked, until I realized where I was and what was occurring. I began to cry uncontrollably, something I've since learned is not unusual for a person coming out of anesthesia. My chest felt like it had been run over by a semi, and tubes were sticking out of my nose, my throat, my ribs, my back. Every breath produced pain, and my head spun like a merry-go-round. It was as though someone had swung a large sledgehammer and hit me squarely in the head.

My arm seemed to weigh a ton as I lifted it, and all the needles and tubes stuck in it, to my eyes to wipe away the tears. I pressed the button to summon a nurse, but no one came. It was difficult to see without my glasses, but I thought the clock on the wall read 6:30. That was the same time I had gone into surgery. There had been a whirl of activity as they wheeled me into the operating room, but now I saw no one. I glanced through the open door of the dark recovery room to the lighted hall, deserted, empty. I pressed the button again. Eternity. I tried to call out, but my lungs were too weak.

> **Words from one of my own sermons came back to me: "You'll never know that Jesus is all you need until Jesus is all you have."**

"Jesus, Jesus, Jesus," I repeated inside my soul.

"There's just something about that name!" sang my soul, recalling the words to a Bill Gaither song I'd sung in church a thousand times. My soul continued to sing: "Sweetest Rose of Sharon, came to set us free, Jesus, Jesus, He's everything to me, yes, He's all the world to me."

Words from one of my own sermons came back to me: "You'll never know that Jesus is all you need until Jesus is all you have."

Never Utterly Alone

That entire episode ran across my mind in a split second as I heard Vern cry over the phone line a thousand miles away in New York.

"Have you ever felt real lonely, Mr. Doud?" Vern asked again.

"Yes, sir, I have. But I realize now that even when I felt totally alone, I wasn't alone. You feel lonely, Vern, but you are not alone. Just pause and know Christ's presence. He is with you. Even though we walk through the valley of the shadow of death, He is with us. Be still and know His presence, Vern."

Come Out of the Cave

My recovery from surgery was slower than I expected. To this day, over three years later, I can still feel soreness in the ribs that were surgically severed to reach my stomach and esophagus. Nevertheless, the surgery was a total success, as I have not experienced any other stomach problems and have not had any heartburn or experienced any reflux since the day the surgery took place.

During my physical recovery from surgery, I had hours and hours to lie in bed and think, or pray, and sleep and dream. Inactivity allowed me no escape from the reality of my situation: I was divorced, without a helpmate, and feeling more dependent on God than at any other time in my life. I now realize that was a good thing. My independent nature is what got me in trouble in the first place. Now I felt myself at a place where I had no choice but to get in the wheelbarrow, realizing I couldn't go it alone.

> **When first released from the hospital, I couldn't even bend over and tie my shoes.**

Admitting Dependence

It is very difficult for someone like me who grew up believing "God helps those who help themselves" to finally admit he is helpless. When first released from the hospital, I couldn't even bend over and tie my shoes. I had to have help to put on a coat, sit up in bed, or get out of a chair. My attempts at independence produced physical pain, and I realized my stubborn indepen-

163

dence in life had produced much emotional and spiritual pain.

I remembered my father again, quoting what he said was his favorite Bible verse: "God helps those who help themselves." And I knew my father wasn't alone in his belief in this well-known statement. My dad found it hard to believe when I told him his cherished verse was not biblical at all, but rather expressed a belief that is quite contrary to the biblical view of man—helpless without God's help. "'God helps those who realize they can't help themselves,' would be a better way of putting it," I had told my dad. I don't think I ever really believed that until I found myself totally helpless and at the mercy of others.

> **I spent more time thinking than I did praying, and the result was a renewed determination to "fix my situation" whatever the cost.**

One of my cherished friends came all the way from Pennsylvania to spend a few days taking care of me. His wife and children back in Grove City gave their blessing so Steve could come and cook and clean. Kindness like this was hard for me to accept. Steve even scrubbed my kitchen floor on his hands and knees, and I felt so unworthy of such a gift and sacrifice.

Folks from my church, and other friends, took turns making meals and doing my laundry. Tammy kept the kids until I was able to take care of them again. Little by little I regained my strength, and, unfortunately, my stubbornness.

Slipping Back into Denial and Self-pity

I spent more time thinking than I did praying, and the result was a renewed determination to "fix my situation" whatever the cost. In other words, I regressed back to living in denial, not accepting my divorce and the losses which had occurred in my life. Ironically, I felt a certain pride in feeling this way: "God must be proud of me for not giving up!" In a way I felt God had failed to save my marriage, and consequently, it was now up to me to turn tragedy into victory.

Denial often includes pretending things are not what they actually are. When I resumed my speaking schedule, I faced a challenge each time I went out to speak. People asked about my family, and I answered concerning my children and then tried to change the subject before they could ask about my wife. Often, however, the truth surfaced, and when it did I wanted to hide from the reality of it and continue to live as though everything was unchanged.

People who experience deep regret, the pain of divorce, the death of a loved one, or some other loss, all encounter the various stages of grief. Denial is a stage of grief difficult to transcend. Many people get stuck in their denial and find it hard to move on.

After surgery I tried to get back to life as usual, but the problem was "usual" didn't exist anymore. Life was a whole new ball game, with a different opponent, unfamiliar rules, and an uncharted course. Quite honestly, I just wanted to go to bed and never get up, to be saved the daunting task of learning to cope with life in an entirely new way.

> **Surely God would understand if I just gave up.**

Life seemed so unfair. I had fought so many battles, enough I thought to win the war, but now I felt as though the war had just begun and my arsenal had been destroyed. A few years earlier, standing in the White House with my wife and the President of the United States of America, I felt atop the world, high on a mountain, the valley far below. But now, physically weak, emotionally exhausted, spiritually drained, I crawled to the bottom of a deep valley, unable even to see the summit of the mountain I had transcended.

Surely God would understand if I just gave up.

I canceled speaking engagements; I shut myself off from others; I wallowed in self-pity; I resigned from the ministry; I felt like resigning from life.

The board of elders at my church accepted my resignation, but God didn't, and neither did my closest friends.

Elijah's Example

I took comfort in reading and rereading the story of Elijah. Perhaps the most famous and dramatic of God's prophets, Elijah knew both victory and defeat, and he experienced both mountaintops and dark caves.

The account of Elijah's story in 1 Kings 18-19 is dramatic and filled with practical application for our lives today. Elijah stood alone at Mount Carmel against 450 prophets of Baal and 400 prophets of Asherah. These false prophets called out to their god, but their god did not answer. Elijah alone took a stand for the Lord, and the Lord our God answered from heaven with flashing fire. Elijah killed all the false prophets and knew great victory, but soon he would exchange the victory on the mountaintop for a cave in the wilderness.

King Ahab reported to Queen Jezebel what Elijah had done. Jezebel angrily promised Elijah: "You killed my prophets, and now I swear by the gods that I am going to kill you by this time tomorrow night" (1 Kings 19:2, TLB).

Hearing the queen's threat, Elijah escaped to the wilderness where he prayed to God that he would die: "I've had enough. . . . Take away my life. I've got to die sometime, and it might as well be now" (1 Kings 19:4, TLB).

Ever feel like that, dear reader? The only thing that kept me from feeling exactly the same way was my four children, whom I realized needed me more than I needed them. Nevertheless, I could identify with Elijah and understood his prayer. Elijah had had enough. He wanted to quit. Give up. Resign. End it. Finish. Call it off. Escape from it all. So what did he do? He lay down and went to sleep!

I did the same exact thing. I slept fourteen to sixteen hours a day and wished I could sleep more. I had somewhat of an excuse:

I had sleep apnea and was making up for years of interrupted sleep. But sleep was really an escape from reality.

Elijah slept and slept until an angel woke him up and told him to eat. Elijah awakened, ate, and then went back to sleep. I had many days just like that. The only thing I seemed to accomplish was eating and sleeping. The angel woke Elijah up again, and again instructed him to eat. "You still have a long journey ahead of you," the angel told Elijah.

Elijah's Cave Retreat

Even though Elijah thought he was at the end, he wasn't. A long journey still lay ahead. I've known many people who live as if they've reached the end of their journey. I was speaking with a young friend earlier this week who at the age of thirty-four already felt as though the best years of his life were behind him. God has to shake my friend up and let him know that there is still a long journey ahead of him, and that the best is yet to come.

Likewise, God had to wake me up and tell me to get out of bed. He wasn't finished with me yet either.

Elijah arose, traveled for a while, but then retreated into a cave. People recovering from feelings of regret, despair, fear, and depression must surface occasionally, but they often retreat quickly, and hide like Elijah in their makeshift caves of isolation.

Elijah cried to God to take his life, but instead God came to Elijah in the cave, and asked him: "What are you doing here, Elijah?" (1 Kings 19:9, TLB)

Elijah used this opportunity to unload a ton of regretful feelings on God. "You know what I'm doing in here, God. I've worked my butt off for You! I stood up for You when no one else would! I always worried about doing the right thing and tried to put Your will ahead of my own! And what reward do I get? They are searching for me and trying to kill me! After all I've done, this is the thanks I get! All those people who turned their backs on You are better off than I am! I don't get it. I give up!"

My paraphrase above might be slightly exaggerated, but I don't think so. Read and study Elijah's conversation with God, and I think you'll find the above sentiment accurately expresses how Elijah felt.

The story gets even more dramatic. Elijah continued to hide in the cave, isolated from the rest of the world. A mighty windstorm struck the mountain cave, dislodging huge boulders, but Elijah didn't budge. The windstorm was followed by an earthquake and then a fire. Still Elijah didn't budge. But then God gently whispered, and Elijah heard His voice and arose and stood at the entrance of the cave.

"Why are you here, Elijah?" God asked.

Again, Elijah unloaded: "I have been working very hard for the Lord God of the armies of heaven, but the people have broken their covenant and have torn down Your altars; they have killed every one of Your prophets except me; and now they are trying to kill me too" (1 Kings 13-14, TLB).

I think it is interesting God spoke to Elijah with a whisper, rather than through the wind, an earthquake, or fire. Thankfully Elijah recognized God's voice.

God often speaks in a gentle whisper to a receptive, heart. Many people seem to think God speaks mainly in grandiose ways. They want to see spectacular miracles or attend huge conferences to feel close to God. Elijah's story reminds us that God is often best heard when we slow down our busy lives and stop to listen. God often speaks in a gentle whisper to a receptive, humble heart.

God's Whispered Promises

I started to think of all the ways God was whispering to me: the shoeshine man in Las Vegas who told me "Jesus Still Loves Me"; the notes and pictures and hugs and kisses from my children; a friend who came all the way from Pennsylvania to help take care of me; friends who came to cook and clean my house; the ability to read the Word of God and talk to God in prayer; the gifts of renewed health and prosperity. The more I listened, the more I could hear God's voice in the simple everyday occurrences I just took for granted.

I could hear God saying: "Guy, I haven't given up on you. I still have work for you to do. Get up. Get out of bed. The best is yet to come!"

Elijah had complained to God about being the only one in Israel who had remained faithful to God. But God informed Elijah that there were over 7,000 other men who had been faithful too. Strange. Over 7,000 faithful followers, but Elijah thought he was the only one. This is a good example of the harmful effect of self-pity. It zaps our passion and discounts the good we've done. Feeling sorry for ourselves is a real joy stealer.

If you feel you are the only one who is suffering so, just take a minute and look around. If you think you're the only one remaining faithful, just take a minute and look around. Others carry heavy burdens too, and there is a sizable remnant of God's people who remain faithful.

God understood Elijah's feelings, and He understood mine too. He understands yours also. Regret, disappointments, defeat, depression, all leave us strumming the heartstring of self-pity. But God whispers to us, "Get up and get going! Come out of the cave!"

Getting in Touch with Anger and Letting Go

It is up to you to decide whether or not to come out of your cave and get on with your life. Friends may be encouraging you, and God may be whispering or even yelling to you, but the decision is yours to make. I wanted someone to make the decision for me.

Self-pity, regret, bitterness, all disable us and render us nearly useless. We will remain stuck, hiding in the cave of solitude, until we choose to get up and come out.

I actually resented it when I learned I was responsible for me. Such responsibility meant I was unable to blame anyone else. And I loved to play the blame game. I even blamed God for the lack of joy in my life. It made me angry to think I had to shoulder the responsibility for my life.

Examining My Anger

From childhood onward we all know we have certain rights We have basic rights guaranteed by the Constitution of the United States: the right to life, liberty, and the pursuit of happiness. We have personal rights: the right to be treated as an individual, and the right to make our own decisions about what is best for our lives. Often, however, we feel our rights have been violated. This produces anger.

> **It made me angry to think I had to shoulder the responsibility for my life.**

Anger in and of itself is not wrong. Anger is neutral. In fact, recognizing our anger is healthy. The Bible says: "Be angry, but sin not" (Ephesians 4:26). The problem comes when our anger leads to sin. It is essential, therefore, for us to identify our anger and deal with it constructively.

Again, I'll use myself as an example. Looking back at my life, what occurrences made me angry? I thought long and hard. The first hurdle was to break my denial and accept the fact I was angry. What did I have to be angry about?

I wrote in my journal:

My doctor says he thinks I have a lot of repressed anger, and I should try to identify it. But I've never thought of myself as an angry person. As I look back at my childhood, I guess I'm angry I was sick so much, missing almost a whole year of school. I wanted to be good at sports, but instead I was on crutches and had to deal with deteriorating joints and constant pain. It didn't seem fair to me. And speaking of fair, why couldn't I have born into a family with an active metabolism? I never ate that much, but my 'cute baby fat' became layered adult fat, and my obesity caused a lot of heartache.

I was always self-conscious about my fat and always felt on the outside looking in. I remember taking thumbtacks and poking them into my fat thighs, hoping my self-punishment would be sentence enough, and I wouldn't have to bear the punishment of others.

I remember lying to my neighborhood friends, telling them I was going on a trip to California to visit my aunt and uncle, when I really just stayed at home and hid for almost two weeks. I wanted some experience to compare with their stories about going on vacation, or going to their lake cabins. I wanted to feel like one of the guys, but in comparing myself with them, I never seemed to match up.

As I wrote in my journal, I couldn't believe how much anger I'd repressed. I was angry at my father who was uninvolved in my life. I was angry at my mother who was nervous and sick so much of the time. I was angry at myself for being fat. I was angry at my arthritis. I was angry at God for not improving my lot in life. I was very angry.

For the most part, I had stuffed my anger deep inside, believing it a sin to show it. *A good Christian like me shouldn't be angry,* I thought.

What happens to anger turned inward? It festers. It seethes. It is a volcano waiting to erupt. It bubbles with bitterness, and causes deep, dark depression.

I thought expressing my anger with a show of emotion would be sinful. I knew it would be wrong to lash out, throw a chair across the room, resort to temper tantrums or name calling, or seek revenge. But I didn't realize at first that "stuffing" the anger, repressing it, was just as destructive. Repressed anger rots away and destroys one's spirit, thereby damaging communication with God.

Anger and Selfishness

Just as loneliness often results from selfishness, anger often results from preconceived ideas concerning what we believe to be our rights. One of the hardest things about being a Christian is being "in the world" but not being "of it." When we are "of the world," we conform to the world's set of standards. Selfishness is one of the world's primary standards.

"Look out for number one!" "Me first!" "You deserve the best!" "Don't let anyone stand in your way!" There almost seems to be something noble about

> **Repressed anger rots away and destroys one's spirit, thereby damaging communication with God.**

these statements, but when everyone has a similar philosophy, it doesn't take too long before individuals collide in their selfish pursuits. The collisions occur in family relationships. Individuals smack together on the job. Some relational crashes in the church end up dividing entire church families. Nations often end up at war, each fighting for their perceived list of rights. Whose needs come first?

This isn't the way God intended it. Romans 12 demonstrates practically how the children of God should live in the world. Paul writes:

> And so, dear brothers, I plead with you to give your bodies to God. Let them be a living sacrifice, holy—the kind He can accept. When you think of what He has done for you, is this too much to ask? Don't copy the behavior and customs of this world, but be a new and different person with a fresh newness in all you do and think. Then you will learn from your own experience how His ways will really satisfy you (Romans 12: 1-2, TLB).

God's Way Versus the World's Way

God's ways are so different from the world's way. The world says, "Think of yourself first." God says, "Give yourself up as a sacrifice."

A few nights ago I ordered pizza to be delivered to the house. Seth had said he wasn't hungry, and I didn't feel hungry, so I only ordered one pizza for the five of us instead of the usual two. When the pizza arrived, however, Seth found his appetite, and the smell of the fresh, hot pizza started my stomach growling. Suddenly, the pizza was almost gone, and we were fighting over who got the last two pieces.

One of my children said to his siblings: "I should get the pizza because I'm bigger than you." One of the others answered: "I should get it because it was my idea to order it." And of course, I could have added, "I should get it because I paid for it." We each had our perception of our rights. The problem was there was only so much pizza, not enough for everyone to be completely satisfied. So whose needs should triumph?

It is rather a funny analogy, but life is like one big pizza. The hungry throngs all grab for what they perceive to be their share. If their individual needs are not met, people often get angry and attack those whom they believe denied them their rights. This is the world's way, but God has a better idea. God says: "Don't copy the behavior and customs of this world, but be a new and different person" (Romans 12:2).

The pizza problem was settled easily enough. Like most parents would, I sacrificed my demand for more, and found something else for Seth and me to eat, since we were the ones who hadn't planned on eating any pizza. I sliced the remaining two pieces into smaller pieces, and when everyone had had their fill, there was still one piece remaining.

Some people incorrectly believe sacrifice means allowing others to walk over them. It does not. You don't have to be a doormat. You do have your rights, and God cares about your rights. But often what we perceive to be our rights are nothing more than selfish or perfectionistic demands which would be better off yielded to God.

Paul continues:

> Don't just pretend that you love others: really love them. Hate what is wrong. Stand on the side of the good. Love each other with brotherly affection and take delight in honoring each other. . . .
>
> Be patient in trouble, and prayerful always. When God's children are in need, you be the one to help them out. And get into the habit of inviting guests home for dinner or, if they need lodging, for the night.
>
> If someone mistreats you because you are a

Christian, don't curse him; pray that God will bless him. When others are happy, be happy with them. If they are sad, share their sorrow. Work happily together. Don't try to act big. Don't try to get into the good graces of important people, but enjoy the company of ordinary folks. And don't think you know it all! (Romans 12:9-16, TLB)

These verses get to the heart of the matter concerning our personal responsibility as Christians. Many Christians avoid worldly vices yet still maintain a worldly attitude. We probably all know "Christians" who are arrogant, selfish, stubborn, and proud. God wants to give us a whole new mind and a whole new attitude.

As I examined my anger, I discovered most of it springs from selfishness. A case in point. It is a Sunday afternoon in December, and I am watching the Minnesota Vikings (I bleed purple) play their arch rival, the Green Bay Packers (Cheeseheads that they are). The Vikes have the ball at the Pack one-yard line. It is fourth and goal. The Vikes go to the line; our quarterback calls out the play; the telephone rings; I answer it quickly and someone with a fakey cheerful voice who can't even pronounce my name asks me if I want to renew the warranty on my washing machine.

Suddenly, I'm angry. Do I have a right to be angry? Yes. Do I have a right to allow my anger to cause me to sin? No.

Another case in point. I return home late from a speaking engagement. I feel I desperately need to sleep in in the morning, so I turn off the phone beside my bed. I am awakened after only a couple hours of sleep by one of my children who hands me the portable phone from downstairs and says: "You have a phone call, Dad."

There is a natural part of me that wants to yell and say: "You know I got home very late; why didn't you take a message and let me sleep!" In my "perfect" world my sleep would not have been interrupted, and I would always get to see every play of every Vikings game. In my perfect world I'd be happily married. In my perfect world the kids would always clean up their messes, it would never rain when I want to play golf, all the pictures I take would be in focus, I wouldn't struggle with allergies, flight attendants would always be cheerful, all planes would depart and arrive on time, I'd only have to mow the grass once each summer, the snow wouldn't fall on my driveway or sidewalk, I would win the Publisher's Clearing House Sweepstakes. . . .

> **When anger arises because of unrealistic, perfectionistic expectations, it is not valid anger, and we need to let it go.**

Get my drift? Much, if not most of our anger stems from the expectations we have of how things should be. When things don't turn out as we think they should, definite feelings arise. One such feeling is regret, and another is anger. When anger arises because of unrealistic, perfectionistic expectations, it is not valid anger, and we need to let it go.

Letting Anger Go

How do you let anger go? First, recognize your anger. Put it into words that are factual and to the point:

I am upset you promised to call but never did.

I am angry and hurt you are spreading rumors about me.

There is no need to attack someone, simply state how you feel. It is difficult for others to disagree with how you feel. They may not understand your feelings, but if you state them in a factual manner, it is almost impossible for other people to deny them.

If possible, directly confront the person or persons whom you feel offended you. Avoid attacking them, or indicating you plan to get revenge or retaliate.

A few years ago one of my children came home from school crying. He explained that the teacher had humiliated him in front of the entire class. My Irish temper flared quickly, and I was ready to go to the school and challenge the teacher to a shootout. As my son explained his perception of what happened, I became angrier and angrier, and I began to feel the teacher should be fired or at least sentenced to prison. In my perfect world, no child should ever be treated like this.

Fortunately, through many experiences, I have come to recognize my anger and handle it more appropriately. It doesn't do any good to pretend I am not angry when I am. No, anger must be confronted.

After listening to my son, I prayed and asked God to help handle my anger in a constructive way. Then I phoned the teacher, and surprisingly, he was expecting to get a call from me. He admitted he had lost his temper and apologized, explaining to me that he would apologize to my son as well. My son had done something he shouldn't have done, but the teacher reacted in a way he shouldn't have. Both were at fault.

This is often the case when anger takes charge. We sacrifice rational thought and sensibility, and chaos results. It is like a riot breaking out. The rioters often have a justifiable reason for their anger, but they display it inappropriately, which often results in inappropriate attempts to subdue it. Next thing you know the neighborhood is in flames; people have lost control.

A long list of regrets can turn into a heart full of bitterness ready to erupt in anger. Those of us who have "renewed minds"— the mind of Christ—must bring our regrets, our bitterness, and our anger to the Cross and allow them to be crucified with Christ. We must surrender our "right" to get even or seek revenge, for God says:

Never pay back evil for evil. Do things in such a way that everyone can see you are honest clear through. Don't quarrel with anyone. Be at peace with everyone, just as much as possible.

Dear friends, never avenge yourselves. Leave that to God, for He has said that He will repay those who deserve it (Romans 12:17-19, TLB).

We can best deal with our anger, which originates because of our expectations and selfishness, by simply letting it go. The child who awoke me with the phone in his hand did so because he thought he was being helpful. The woman who called to see if I want to renew my warranty was only doing her job. We gain nothing by reacting to such situations in anger. No one has purposely offended us. Consequently, there is no one to confront. Let it go. Let God. When you do this, your anger soon dissipates. Choosing to hold on to anger only makes you angrier and more frustrated.

Consciously give your anger to God.

But what about justifiable anger? Let's say someone threw eggs at your car, or deliberately used a tool or key to put big scratches in your car? What if someone broke into your house and stole your wallet and credit cards and your car keys and your car? What if someone spread malicious, untrue rumors about you, trying to destroy your reputation? What if someone you trusted with all your heart betrayed you? What if you were denied what is rightfully yours?

Consciously give your anger to God.

All of the above has happened to me. Do I have a right to be angry? You bet I do. But what should I do about my anger?

Seek revenge? No.

Respond in kind? No.

Stuff the anger down inside and fail to deal with it? No! Identify and admit the feelings I have and ask God to take charge? Yes. This is what God would have us do with our regret and angry feelings. In fact, God tells us to take it even one step further:

> Don't take the law into your own hands. Instead, feed your enemy if he is hungry. If he is thirsty give him something to drink and you will be 'heaping coals of fire on his head.' In other words, he will feel ashamed of himself for what he has done to you. Don't let evil get the upper hand but conquer evil by being good (Romans 12: 19-21).

Such behavior sounds almost impossible to me, and it is. But it is not impossible for the Holy Spirit. In the next chapter we will discuss how we have to rely on a power greater than our own to overcome the regret, depression, and anger that would infect our lives and steal our joy.

What We Can Change

When our attempts fail to control all the circumstances of life, and we realize our idea of a perfect world will never be, we become angry and depressed. Letting go and letting God simply involves asking God for the wisdom to know the difference between the things we can change and the things we can't. Those things we can change, God will give us the power to change. The things we can't change are best surrendered to God. The well-known Serenity Prayer expresses this truth so simply:

> God, grant me the serenity to
> accept the things I cannot change;
> the courage to change the things I can;
> and the wisdom to know the difference.

God has promised wisdom to all those who ask. He keeps His

promises.

If you are like me, dear one, not only do you wish to change many of life's circumstances, but you probably also have a laundry list of people you'd like to change. In my book *Joy in the Journey* I tell the story of how I came to learn a slightly different version of the Serenity Prayer, called the Codependent's Prayer. It goes like this:

God, grant me the serenity to
accept the things I cannot change;
the courage to change the people I can;
and the wisdom to know that person is me.

I can't change the fact Tammy decided to end our marriage. I can't change the fact both my parents died at early ages. I can't change the fact I was raised in a dysfunctional home. I can't change the fact I made some very poor decisions in the past. I can't change the fact I have allowed my temper to rage out of control at times.

> **When we make conscious decisions, when we choose to do it God's way, we are transformed in a radical way.**

I can choose, however, to forgive—to forgive others and myself. I can choose to turn my anger over to God and let it go. I can choose to stop and seek God's plan and purpose in every situation. I can choose to allow the grace of God to comfort me in whatever circumstance I'm in because His grace is sufficient.

When we make conscious decisions, when we choose to do it God's way, we are transformed in a radical way. Our minds are renewed. Our spirits are lifted. We have a whole new way of looking at life's circumstances. We go from crying out like Christ on the cross: "My God, My God, why have You forsaken Me?"

(Matthew 27:46) to echoing Christ's last cry: "Father, into Your hands I commit My spirit" (Luke 23:46).

Regrets. Anger turned inward, unresolved, festering away. Depression. Joy stolen. Lives regretfully lived and unfulfilled.

Dear one, God understands. Get in touch with your regrets and your anger, and give them to God.

When you empty your regrets and surrender your anger to God, He quickly moves into the empty spaces with additional love and grace.

Live beyond regret.

A Whole New Way
of Thinking

How many times have you heard someone say "Let go and let God"? I had at least a hundred people tell me that is what I needed to do. And I've told at least a hundred people that letting go and letting God is what they need to do. The problem was I wasn't really sure how to let go.

What does it really mean to "let go and let God"?

No Formula to Follow

As a pastor, counseling hundreds of sincere people who really desire to trust and obey, I realize most of them don't really know how to do what they long to do. They say a prayer. They come to the altar. They have good intentions. But then they find themselves in situation after situation where they perform in ways unpleasing to themselves and to God. The result is more regret, feelings of failure, defeat, discouragement, depression, and eventually resignation.

> **What does it really mean to "let go and let God"?**

I remember one person telling me: "I tried the Jesus thing and it didn't work."

If you examine his statement, you see that this person believed, as many people do, that there is a formula to follow and if we follow it, we should produce the desired results.

Follow this diet and lose a hundred pounds!

Try this work-out program and firm up your abs!

187

Invest in this money scheme, and you'll be rich!

Let go and let God, and you'll find true happiness in life!

Most people assume letting go and letting God involves going to church, following the Ten Commandments, doing the right things, saying the right things, and going to the right places. They also assume letting go means not doing certain things as well. If we perform in a particular way, we'll suddenly experience real joy in life, the joy for which we've been searching.

If we had been able to perform correctly, always able to make the right choices, always able to say "no" to temptation, then there would have been no need for the Cross.

We will always be frustrated if our joy is dependent on our performance. If we had been able to perform correctly, always able to make the right choices, always able to say "no" to temptation, then there would have been no need for the Cross. In our flesh "we crucify ourselves between two thieves: regret for yesterday, and fear of tomorrow." When we become Christians, however, we receive the Spirit of Christ, who indwells us. If we continue to live with regret for yesterday, and fear of tomorrow, we are turning our backs on what Christ did for us on the cross.

A Transforming Process

Jesus was crucified so we wouldn't have to be. Therefore, we acknowledge His great sacrifice by allowing His Spirit to give us a whole new mind, a whole new way of thinking. This is the bottom line. We allow Christ to transform and renew our minds by literally choosing to dwell on the things of the Spirit rather than on the things of the flesh.

Many psychologists have made a career of simply telling people to change their "self-talk." Certain doctors claim they invented this method of psychological counseling. The truth is, long ago God, through the inspiration of His Spirit, instructed us to change our "self-talk" by renewing our minds:

Don't copy the behavior and customs of this world, but be a new and different person with a *fresh newness in all you do and think* (Romans 12:2, TLB, emphasis mine).

I emphasize *"fresh newness in all you do and think"* because I want to point out what I believe God is saying: *"I can give you a whole new way of thinking. And a whole new way of thinking will produce a whole new way of doing. And a whole new way of doing means you'll experience a whole new way of living."*

So, the phrases "letting go and letting God," "trusting Jesus," "trying God," all mean being "transformed by the renewing of our minds."

This transformation isn't instantaneous. God doesn't suddenly take over our lives and make us robots who perform exactly the way He wants us to perform. God loves us so much He gives us the freedom to choose to reject Him if we so desire. If He forced us to love Him and follow Him, we wouldn't be human, and love would not exist. Love is a choice. The more we choose to love God, the more our minds our transformed.

Transformation is a process. That is why we refer to the Christian life as a "walk." We do not immediately arrive at our destination, but as we walk with Christ, day by day, we can choose to see things the way He sees them. The more we look at life with Christ's eyes, the more our lives will be transformed and our minds will be renewed.

Mental Choices

Many people have sincerely invited Christ into their hearts, but have not invited Him into their minds. God's Word tells us that King David was a "man after God's own heart," and yet this man "after God's own heart" committed adultery and murder.

I believe David didn't fail because his heart wasn't in the right place, but rather because his mind wasn't in the right place. By reading the Psalms he wrote, we know David loved God and desired to follow Him. We also know David agonized over his failures and his sin. What caused David to sin was what he had chosen to think about. Even though in his heart he knew adultery and murder were wrong, his mind was able

Many people have sincerely invited Christ into their hearts, but have not invited Him into their minds.

to put his heart on hold and his actions soon followed the desire of his mind rather than the desire of his heart.

I've loved Jesus since I was a child. I committed my heart and life to Him when I stood at the front of the Staples Theater after the Billy Graham movie, "The Restless Ones." I asked Jesus to come into my life, and I know He did. I know my name is written in the Lamb's Book of Life, and I know some day when I die, or if before my death He should come again, I will be with Him in glory forever.

Nonetheless, I believe Jesus loves me so much He didn't turn me into a robot and take away my ability to choose. I still have my mind, and like David I can choose to dwell on some pretty ugly things.

When wronged, I can choose to think about revenge and retaliation, rather than think about forgiveness.

When tempted, I can choose to pursue the desires of my flesh rather than think about godly things.

Consider this example. Have you ever watched Robin Leach's program on television, "The Lifestyles of the Rich and Famous"? Well, I have, and I have to admit that more than once I've found myself envying the material possessions of others. Wouldn't it be great to have several homes throughout the world? A villa on the Riviera . . . a private jet to whisk you across the Atlantic . . . servants to prepare your food and clean your house and make your bed. . . .

Even as I think such thoughts, I envision the picture of a child sent to me from Compassion International. The child in this picture simply wants a chance to live, to have food to eat, a place to sleep, perhaps the opportunity to go to school and to receive health care when needed.

I am ashamed I allowed such envy in my life, and I have asked God to forgive me for it. And God does forgive. He is able to do even more than forgive, however. He is able to give me a whole new way of thinking.

Thinking That Depends on the Cross

Let me stress this: **our new way of thinking is made possible not because of what we did or can do; our new way of thinking is made possible because of what Jesus did on the cross.**

When we ask Christ to be Lord and Savior in our lives and acknowledge His death on the cross, something extraordinary happens: our relationship to sin is forever changed. We are no longer guilty because of original sin—our debt to sin was paid by Christ on the cross. Paul, in Romans, likens original sin to slavery. He writes: "In those days when you were slaves of sin you didn't bother much with goodness" (Romans 6:20, TLB).

When you choose to accept Christ, see what happens: "But now you are free from the power of sin" (Romans 6:22, TLB).

It is an amazing transformation! Read more about what happens:

Your old sin-loving nature was buried with Him by baptism when He died, and when God the Father, with glorious power, brought Him back to life again, you were given His wonderful new life to enjoy.

For you have become a part of Him, and so you died with Him, so to speak, when He died; and now you share His new life, and shall rise as He did. Your old evil desires were nailed to the cross with Him; that part of you that loves to sin was crushed and fatally wounded, so that your sin-loving body is no longer under sin's control, no longer needs to be a slave to sin; for when you are deadened to sin you are freed from all its allure and its power over you. And since your old sin-loving nature "died" with Christ, we know that you will share His new life. Christ rose from the dead and will never die again. Death no longer has any power over Him. He died once for all to end sin's power, but now He lives forever in unbroken fellowship with God. So look upon your old sin nature as dead and unresponsive to sin, and instead be alive to God, alert to Him, through Jesus Christ our Lord (Romans 6:4–11, TLB).

We've been liberated from sin! We've been set free from the chains that bound us to a sinful nature! What has made this freedom possible? Nothing that we've done, but Christ's death on the cross.

Unfortunately, so many Christians never truly appreciate the totality of God's grace. Many continue to work to try to earn their salvation. For them, salvation comes by jumping through all the right hoops. Consequently, when they miss a hoop or two, they feel defeated, deflated, and resigned.

Understanding God's grace means we don't have to feel defeated. Even though we lose a battle now and then, we have the confidence of knowing that Christ has already won the war! Of course, this doesn't mean we can plan to sin, or try to fail, but it does allow for our human frailties and our minds that sometimes wander and focus on sinful things.

Again, the mind is key. All sin begins first as a thought. We choose to either focus on the sin, or to think about spiritual things. Many times we don't even realize we have a choice, but we always do. Paul offers insight into this as well:

> Those who let themselves be controlled by their lower natures live only to please themselves, but those who follow after the Holy Spirit find themselves doing those things that please God. Following after the Holy Spirit leads to life and peace, but following after the old nature leads to death (Romans 8:5-6, TLB).

The Affect of Our Mental Choices

We are the ones who decide which nature will control us. We have two choices: our new spiritual nature which is ours in Christ, or our lower, selfish nature. And understand this: the more we choose to think about spiritual things, the more spiritual we will become. And the more we choose to think about fleshly things, the more fleshly we will become. This is why Scripture emphatically demands:

All sin begins first as a thought.

> And now, brothers, as I close this letter, let me say this one more thing: Fix your thoughts on what is true and good and right. Think about things that are pure and lovely, and dwell on the fine, good things in others. Think about all you can praise God for and be glad about (Philippians 4:8, TLB).

One of the greatest truths I've learned is this: **Victory over sin, negativity, depression, and regret is most easily won at the thought level.** I sin only after I think about sinning. I become negative and filled with regret only after I choose to dwell on negative and regretful things. Instead, I can choose to dwell, and you can choose to dwell, "on the fine good things," and "all we can praise God for and be glad about."

Every thought is capable of sending our minds along paths of envy, lust, greed, regret, and sin. Therefore, every thought must be captured, surrendered, and turned over to Christ. Ours is a spiritual battle, and God has given us a mighty weapon. Paul puts it this way:

> For though we live in the world, we do not wage war as the world does. The weapons we fight with are not the weapons of the world. On the contrary, they have divine power to demolish strongholds. We demolish arguments and every pretension that sets itself up against the knowledge of God, and we take captive every thought to make it obedient to Christ (2 Corinthians 10: 3-5).

We take every thought captive! **This is the key to living beyond regret.** This is the key to living as a child of God. It means we put on a new mind, the mind of Christ, and when we face difficult circumstances, we ask ourselves: "What would Jesus do?"

Like me, you may have experienced, or will experience some very painful circumstances in life. Your spouse may leave you; one of your children may die; you may be unjustly accused of something you didn't do; you may lose your job; you may make some very bad decisions and allow your mind to dwell on ungodly things. BUT, God has given you the ultimate weapon: a whole new mind with a whole new way of thinking.

When Christ hung on the cross, He could have said: "Father, I want you to send 10,000 angels and destroy those who persecute Me!" Instead, He said: "Father, forgive them for they do not know what they are doing" (Luke 23:34).

In the Upper Room, Jesus could have said to Judas: "I know what you're up to, and believe Me I'll get revenge!" But instead, He said: "What you are about to do, do quickly" (John 13:27).

Instead of allowing our minds to pursue those things that will only bring increased pain and suffering, we must dwell on all the things we can praise God for and be happy about.

When I start to dwell on the things of praise, I am overwhelmed with the multitude of blessings which are mine.

Think on these things! My children, my family, my security, my leisure, my work, and my God!

My God is the God of the entire universe, and yet He is small enough to live within my heart. And He does live there, constantly reminding me that He has chosen me and that I will live forever with Him. He keeps telling me, although sometimes I fail to listen: "Guy, the best is yet to come! The best is yet to come! The best is yet to come!"

Dear one, put on the mind of Christ! Take every thought captive! Live beyond despair and regret! And remember, *the best is yet to come!*

> **Instead of allowing our minds to pursue those things that will only bring increased pain and suffering, we must dwell on all the things we can praise God for and be happy about.**

Kodak Moments

I t has been over four years since the night I came home to an empty house. Much has changed. One thing certain about life, it is forever changing. In our humanness, we sometimes wish we could turn back the clock. Sometimes I'd like to go back to being a child again, leaving all of life's worries to Mom and Dad. I'd like to sit in my father's lap again. I'd give almost anything to have one of Mom's home cooked meals. I even wish I could mow Grandpa's lawn one more time and stop for a glass of Grandma's homemade lemonade.

I'd like to meet the neighbor kids and go out behind Haskin's Gas Station and have a good game of baseball. And there are at least a hundred friends I wish I could call and talk to once again.

And do I need to say it? I wish I could go back to the moment I first realized I loved Tammy, and knowing what I know now, do many things so differently. I am, after all, only human.

> **I can honestly look back at life and thank God for where I've been.**

Does it sound as if my life is filled with a ton of regret? Well, it isn't. I can honestly look back at life and thank God for where I've been. I look to today and tomorrow and trust God for where I'm going. I truly do believe the best is yet to come.

Realize the Beauty of Life and Change

When I was in college, I played the role of the Stage Manager in Thornton Wilder's famous play *Our Town*. The Stage Manager serves as the narrator of the play. In the last act, Emily,

199

a young married woman who has died giving birth to her first child, approaches the Stage Manager at her graveside and asks if she can go back and live her life over again. The Stage Manager, a transcendent figure as he talks to a dead Emily, tells her she can go back but she shouldn't because the pain would be too much to bear. He tells her that if she goes back and views herself living life, she will be filled with regret because of all the simple joys and pleasures she had overlooked when she was alive.

Emily, however, insists that she wants go back and watch herself live part of her life over again. The Stage Manager obliges, and takes Emily back to the morning of her fourteenth birthday. After only a short time observing herself, Emily realizes that there were so many things in life she took for granted. She asks the Stage Manager: "Does anybody realize the beauty of life while they live it, every, every minute?"

Every night after our stage Emily would ask me, the Stage Manager, that question, I'd pause and think a moment before delivering the famous line: "No. Saints and poets maybe, they do some."

As an English teacher, I enjoy teaching poetry, especially poems with a *carpe diem* theme. "Seize the day" was and still is a common theme of much poetry. I always love to encourage my students to "gather rosebuds while ye may." It sounds rather simple, but one of the best antidotes to regret is to stop and count your blessings and remember that "the same flower that blooms today, tomorrow will be a dyin'."

Yes, the years bring many changes, but each change is a new adventure. I've often wished I could freeze time. My children are growing up way too fast. Only Zachary sits on my lap these days, and soon he'll be too big. It is exciting to watch them grow and develop.

Being a single parent has been quite a challenge, and yet it has brought me much closer to my children than I would have been otherwise. When Luke said, "Dad, I want poached eggs," I didn't have the slightest idea how to make them. I do now. And then there was the day when Luke said, "Dad, my football pants need sewing." I didn't have the slightest idea how to sew a pair of pants. I do now.

No, there isn't a clear picture of what tomorrow holds, but as a child of God, I do know who holds tomorrow.

> **No, there isn't a clear picture of what tomorrow holds, but as a child of God's, I do know who holds tomorrow.**

The Gift of a Sunset

Although I try to be creative in preparing meals for the kids and me, I do take us all out to eat at least once a week. Not long after Tammy left, I was at home alone with the children. It was one of those nights I decided we needed to "eat out." The kids suggested a restaurant on Gull Lake because it is one of those places where you can pick out your steak or hamburger or chicken and cook it yourself. My kids like grilling their own food.

We finished our cooking and eating, and we were leaving the restaurant and heading back to the car when I saw a huge, golden sun preparing to set at the far end of the lake. The kids were running toward the car when all of a sudden I yelled: "Come here, kids." They stopped, looked at me strangely, but came running to me nevertheless.

"What, Dad?" each child took turns asking.

I gathered them all around me, picked up Zach, and put my arms around Seth, Luke, and Jessica. "Look at the sunset, kids, isn't it beautiful?"

> **"Our Father in heaven loves us, kids, and your father on earth loves you too."**

For a long moment no one spoke as we all stared at the big ball descending behind the lake. "Our Father in heaven loves us, kids, and your father on earth loves you too."

I am not ashamed to admit that tears welled up in my eyes, and for a few moments longer, my kids were unusually silent. Finally, Seth spoke: "Gee, Dad, this is one of those Kodak moments."

Yes, Seth, that was a Kodak moment. And kids, and you readers too, remember life is filled with Kodak moments. Each moment is special. Each one is a gift from God.

Looking Forward to What Lies Ahead

I come to the end of this book, but not to the end of the story. I am excited about what lies ahead, and I know Jesus is in control.

I wish I could sit down with you, and we could talk about your life. Are you paralyzed with regret, or are you powered with passion? Do you realize that no matter what has happened, Jesus still loves you, and He has a wonderful plan and purpose for your life? Have you waved the white flag of surrender and allowed the Holy Spirit to accomplish that which otherwise would have been impossible?

If you've read this book closely, you realize that the Apostle Paul is one of my heroes. In his letter to the church in Philippi, he writes:

> But all these things that I once thought very worthwhile—now I've thrown them all away so that I can put my trust and hope in Christ alone. Yes, everything else is worthless when compared with the priceless gain of knowing Christ Jesus my Lord. I have put aside all else, counting it worth less than nothing, in order that I can have Christ, and become one with Him, no longer counting on being saved by being good enough or by obeying God's laws, but by trusting Christ to save me; for God's way of making us right with

> **Have you waved the white flag of surrender and allowed the Holy Spirit to accomplish that which otherwise would have been impossible?**

Himself depends on faith—counting on Christ alone. Now I have given up everything else—I have found it to be the only way to really know Christ and to experience the mighty power that brought Him back to life again, and to find out what it means to suffer and to die with Him. So, whatever it takes, I will be one who lives in the fresh newness of life of those who are alive from the dead (Philippians 3: 7–11, TLB).

It took divorce, a deep depression, and complete resignation for me to realize, like Paul, that everything "is worthless when compared with the priceless gain of knowing Christ Jesus my Lord."

In this ever-changing world, "Jesus is the same yesterday, today, and forever." And like the world, life is ever changing. I realize there will be additional challenges to come. My struggles are not over. Neither are yours. But with Paul we can say:

> I don't mean to say I am perfect. I haven't learned all I should even yet, but I keep working toward that day when I will finally be all that Christ saved me for and wants me to be.
>
> No, dear brothers, I am still not all I should be but I am bringing all my energies to bear on this one thing: Forgetting the past and looking forward to what lies ahead, I strain to reach the end of the race and receive the prize for which God is calling us up to heaven because of what Christ Jesus did for us (Philippians 3:12–14, TLB).

Wow! That is my favorite passage of Scripture: **"Forgetting the past and looking forward to what lies ahead, I strain to reach the end of the race and receive the prize. . . ."**

And what a prize! Despite all my failures, the ones in the past and the ones to come, Jesus will look me in the eye on that day and say, "Well done, Guy!"

Along with my mom and my dad, and my grandma and my grandpa, and all of my family and friends who know and love Jesus, we will celebrate for eternity in that place where there is no more pain, or sorrow, or divorce, or death.

> **Will you join me in living out the rest of your life with praise rather than regret?**

That is some prize!

Will you join me in the celebration? Will you join me in living out the rest of your life with praise rather than regret? Will you join me in trusting Jesus that the best is yet to come?

> But our homeland is in heaven, where our Savior the Lord Jesus Christ is; and we are looking forward to His return from there. When He comes back He will take these dying bodies of ours and change them into glorious bodies like His own, using the same mighty power that He will use to conquer all else everywhere (Philippians 3:20-21,TLB).

In the same way Paul closed his letter to the Philippians, I close my book to you: God has given us a choice. Choose to dwell on the things of God rather than on the things of earth. Fix your thoughts on those things that are true, and good, and right. Think about all you can praise God for and be glad about!

See you at the party!